ISBN: 978129005773

Published by:
HardPress Publishing
8345 NW 66TH ST #2561
MIAMI FL 33166-2626

Email: info@hardpress.net
Web: http://www.hardpress.net

Library of the Theological Seminary
PRINCETON, N. J.

Library of Dr. A. A. Hodge.   Presented.

Division

Section

Number

AN

HISTORICAL ENQUIRY,

&c. &c.

AN

HISTORICAL ENQUIRY

INTO THE

PROBABLE CAUSES

OF THE

RATIONALIST CHARACTER

LATELY PREDOMINANT

IN THE

Theology of Germany.

TO WHICH IS PREFIXED,

A LETTER FROM PROFESSOR SACK,

UPON THE

REV. H. J. ROSE'S DISCOURSES ON GERMAN PROTESTANTISM

TRANSLATED FROM THE GERMAN.

BY E. B. PUSEY, M.A.

FELLOW OF ORIEL COLLEGE, OXFORD.

LONDON:
PRINTED FOR C. & J. RIVINGTON,
ST. PAUL'S CHURCH-YARD,
AND WATERLOO-PLACE, PALL-MALL.
1828.

TO THE
RIGHT REV. FATHER IN GOD

CHARLES,

LORD BISHOP OF OXFORD,

IN ACKNOWLEDGMENT OF ADVANTAGES DERIVED

FROM HIS PUBLIC AND PRIVATE ASSISTANCE

IN THE COURSE OF THEOLOGICAL STUDY,

AND FROM THE CONTINUED KINDNESS OF PRIVATE INTERCOURSE,

The following Sheets

ARE INSCRIBED

WITH THE SINCEREST GRATITUDE AND RESPECT.

PREFACE.

The relation which the following sheets bear to a work, which has in this country met with considerable approbation, seems to require that a brief explanation be given of the circumstances in which they originated. Mr. Rose's Essay has unquestionably, through the number of facts which it stated, had the merit of introducing the subject of German Theology more extensively before the English, and of furnishing a considerable number of data, from which the character of the late Rationalist Theology might in itself be appreciated. In the mode, however, in which these facts were presented, the Author missed that arrangement of the facts themselves, through which alone it becomes possible to trace the connexion of causes and effects through the whole course of the system described; as well as a due appreciation of the intrinsic and relative importance of those facts. To some of the innovations a degree of weight seemed to be attached, which their relation to the whole compass of the Christian system did not appear to justify: other attempts, which were in themselves justly stigmatized, had either expired as soon as they came into being, or even if they did enjoy a short-lived existence, were, from their nature and the character of their authors, as little entitled to notice, as the ephemeral and contemptible productions of a Carlile or a Hone. It was indeed almost unavoidable, that, without enquiry in the country itself, mistakes must frequently be committed as to the real influence of any instrument, whether a literary production or an institution. The Christian Evidence Society in this country has appeared at first sight to foreigners, who knew only its object, but neither the manner in which it was conducted, nor the little talent by which it was supported, an engine of some magnitude. Of infinitely more importance, however, appeared to be the omission of the history of German Theology previous to the commencement of the crisis described; since, in that previous history, the deepest causes of this crisis must necessarily lie, and without a full knowledge of this, it seemed hopeless to anticipate any satisfactory results. The causes accordingly incidentally assigned in Mr. Rose's work (for his professed object was to give an account of the actual state of Theology, not of the causes in which that state originated), seemed partly inadequate to produce so great a revolution, partly of too negative a character to be entitled to the name. The weight in particular ascribed to the neglect of a controlling superintendance, and of adherence to the letter of the symbolical books, appeared to confound the withdrawing of what are, at the utmost, but means of prevention, with the introduction of a positive agency. Yet the stream must be filled from some other causes than those which merely shake the floodgates by which it is restrained: nor, unless it were thus swelled beyond its usual height, could the mere opening of a free course to its tide produce so extensive and desolating an inundation. Did the removal of these checks necessarily or probably involve the downfall of the religion, which they were employed to fence in, a strong probability would exist against the truth of that religion, which was thus incapable of maintaining, unassisted, its own ground, and of producing an adequate conviction of its divine origin. The question does not here relate to the use of articles, either to restrain individual error, or as the depository of the faith of highly-gifted and enlightened men, with the standard of whose belief it may be beneficial for all to compare the results of their own conviction; but whether any relaxation of the binding force of these articles will produce not merely deviation from their doctrines within the bounds of Christianity, but the abandonment of the principles and the authority of Christianity itself. The affirmative of this question is indeed implied in the conduct and avowed principles of the Church of Rome, but it has, exteriorly to that church, received hitherto only the unwelcome support of Hobbes, and another English deist [1]. Though fully assured of the excellence of Mr. Rose's intentions, the author could not but think, that the view supported in his work involved the abandonment of the fundamental principles of Protestantism, and derogated from the independence and the inherent power of the word of God. That Scripture did need no such adscititious means to preserve generally its healthful truths from such corruption as would neutralize their efficacy, appeared to result from the history of the early Church, in which for above two centuries no symbols were at all received, and even when heretical speculation did render such safe-guards necessary in individual cases, they were extended no further

---

[1] The author believes that he found this theory in Tindal, but cannot at the moment be certain in which of the English deists he met with it.

than the emergency of such cases required; the rest of the body of Christian doctrine was committed to the keeping of unauthoritative tradition, expounding the word of Scripture: that a recurrence to Scripture is sufficient to regenerate the system when corrupted, independent of, or in opposition to, existing symbols, resulted from the various portions of the history of the Reformation. It must be repeated that it is not intended by the maintenance of these views to derogate from the value of articles generally, much less of such, as are drawn up with so much judgment and moderation as our own; their value is certainly very great both to individuals, as presenting a test by which to examine the character of their own faith, and to the Church, as enabling it to exclude those, who depart from the principles upon which itself was founded. The view, in which the author felt it impossible to participate, was not a supposed probability that the Church might suffer from individual deviations, but the supposition that the whole or the greater part of the body must *necessarily* decline, unless it were voluntarily to bind its hands by the resolution never to deviate from the letter of the faith of its earlier state. During a year's residence in Germany, the author found that every class of theologians, with whom he had intercourse, (and among them were men whose deep piety, sound faith, and extensive views excited his veneration,) shared these opinions with regard both to the inadequacy of the causes assigned by Mr. Rose for the deflections of German theology, and to the classes of errors which the Author thought he perceived in it. Aware, however, of the difficulties under which a stranger must always lie in appreciating the extent and influence of any complex state of things, but thoroughly dissatisfied with all the criticisms which had yet appeared in Germany, he applied to the theologian, of whose letter he has here given a translation, for his opinion in writing, as fully as his important avocations permitted, upon the principal points in Mr. Rose's work. An early work, published by that author on the state of English Protestantism, (though circumstances had prevented his becoming so much acquainted as might have been wished with the largest portion of the Episcopal Church) indicated the possession of the talents and religious character requisite for the execution of the task. He performed it with the ready kindness, which the Author gladly acknowledges to have received from him in a gratifying and useful intercourse, and circumstances alone, which it is not necessary to state, have thus long delayed its appearance. In the translation, the principal object has been to render with the utmost faithfulness the meaning of the original, and to this, (as must be necessarily the case in any precise translation from so rich and powerful a language as the German), style has been voluntarily sacrificed. Professor Sack's numerous occupations not allowing him to enter into the other part of the enquiry, the historical causes of the late revolution in German Theology, the Author has attempted a brief sketch, rather with the view of inducing others, whose principal department may lie within the province of ecclesiastical history, to institute a fuller investigation, than with the wish that his own opinions should be adopted. He feels indeed convinced, from his own examination, and from the independent concurrence of some of the most valuable divines in Germany, that conclusions more or less corresponding with these will be the result of a more extensive enquiry; his only object, however, here is, that such an enquiry should be instituted. On this ground it being to him comparatively indifferent, with what reception his own opinions may meet, he will not feel himself under any obligation to maintain them, should they be opposed. Controversy is generally of little advantage to the public, and detrimental to those who engage in it; and the Author will consequently not think it necessary to abandon his pursuits for the ungrateful and unprofitable employment of self-vindication. The removal from any large public library, as well as from the greater portion of his own, during the period in which this Essay was written, has compelled him for the most part to quote mediate authorities only, instead of having recourse to the immediate sources. He has, however, no reason to apprehend from the character of the authors principally used, Weismann, Buddeus, Schröckh, Mosheim, Henke, Vater, Twesten, any incorrectness of the facts adduced. It may perhaps be necessary to state, in order to avoid misconception, that the term " Evangelical" is used in the following sheets according to the phraseology of the German church, to designate the Lutheran body, that of " Reformed" or " Calvinistic" for such as agree in the doctrine of the Lord's supper with ourselves. There remains in conclusion only, to acknowledge with gratitude the assistance derived from the MS. of a German friend, who has carried on the same enquiry, and whom though the Author is not permitted to name, he cannot but express his sincere sense of his kindness, as well as his thankfulness for the advantages, which through that kindness he has been, on many occasions, permitted to enjoy.

CONTENTS.

INTRODUCTORY LETTER BY PROFESSOR SACK.
HISTORICAL ENQUIRY.

Uses, and extent of the Enquiry—Period from which it must be commenced—Causes of the imperfect completion of the Reformation in Germany—External—Internal—Consequent limitation and narrowing of the Lutheran Church—Pernicious effects on the Theology of the 17th century—View of that Theology in its several parts, Scriptural Interpretation, Doctrinal and Moral Theology, Ecclesiastical History, Practical Theology, and dangers to be apprehended from the state of each—General descriptions of it by Spener and Thomasius—Shocks sustained by this system, from the improvement attempted by Calixtus—from the endeavour of Arndt and Spener to restore genuine Christianity—Means employed by Spener—Their influence—Continuation in the school of Halle—its character, institutions, and influence—its inherent liabilities to degenerate—School indirectly produced by it—Opposition to parts of the prevailing system by Arnold and Thomasius—Effects of the Wolfian Philosophy—Review of the state of Theology at the time of the first struggle with Unbelief—External circumstances tending to promote Unbelief—Moral and intellectual character of the age—Influence of Frederic—English and French Unbelievers—Nicolai—Popular Philosophy—Gradual decline of Theology—Influence of Baumgarten, Ernesti, Michaelis; of Semler, Morus, Koppe, &c. of Steinbart—Principal directions of German Theology then coexisting—Exceptions to the general Character—Individuals who prepared for a restoration of Christianity; Lessing, Herder—Opposition to the shallow philosophic-religious system by Kant—Influence of the system of Kant on its positive and negative side, favorable and unfavorable—Influence of the philosophy of Fichte, Schelling, Jacobi—Final formation of Rationalism—Results—Present state of German Theology and Church.

LETTER

FROM

PROFESSOR SACK

TO

THE AUTHOR.

You express a wish, my dear Friend, for my opinion upon Mr. Rose's book " on the state of Religion in Protestant Germany;" and, even at the risk of your occasionally meeting with views and opinions contrary to those to which you are attached, I will give it you; being fully convinced that we are agreed on the main points, and that you are yourself sufficiently acquainted with Germany to enter into the circumstances, which either remove or mitigate the charges of Mr. R. You will allow me in the outset to own to you that a renewed perusal of the work of your countryman excited in me on two accounts a feeling of pain; on the one hand, that so much evil could be said of the Theological Authors of my country, which it is impossible to clear away; on the other, that this was done in a form and manner which could not but produce a confused view and false picture of the state of Germany. Gladly, however, I allow, that a very different mode of judging of German Theology would have given me infinitely deeper pain. I mean such an agreement with the prevailing views of the Rationalist School as would have presented them to the indifferent party in England under the dazzling colors of theological liberality. This would have seemed to me a yet more unnatural violation of the relation in which the English Church (taking the word in its widest sense) is called upon to stand to the German;

and since Mr. R. has missed the real course of the developement of the opinions of theological Germany, the harsh and oft perplexing manner in which he has delivered his statement may still indirectly be productive of much good, although indeed in order to its attainment much accurate investigation and renewed examination on both sides will be unquestionably indispensable. You will have already perceived, (and indeed you were before aware) that I am not one of those Germans who have received this English work with a mere tissue of revilings, with renewed expressions of self-approbation, altogether mistaking the, (as I do not doubt) excellent and Christian disposition of its author. Very different are the thoughts to which it has given rise in myself; the most essential of these I will endeavour briefly to lay before you.

First, then, I would remark the erroneousness and injustice of the imputation, that the Protestant Churches of Germany, founded as they were on the authority of Holy Scripture, at the same time permitted any one of their ministers and teachers to vary from it even in their public instruction as far and as often as they pleased*. At no place and at no time was such the case. The Protestant Churches of Germany have founded their public teaching and observances on confessions of faith, which their abandonment of unchristian errors compelled them to frame; and in these scriptural "confessions" themselves were marked out the limits, beyond which the liberty of their ministers was not to be extended.

It was unavoidable and it was right, that the period, in which an undue value was attached to the letter of these confessions, should be followed by another, in which a distinction should be made between that which constitutes their essential import (to meet each error by the positive statement of the opposed truth,) and that which in the form of ex-

* P. 10.

pression originated solely in the then state of doctrinal science; nor did this in any way destroy the right and duty to bind down the public teacher to the matter of the confession; nor did the conduct of individuals who, in literary controversy, when this difference had been perceived, spoke slightingly of the value of the confessions generally, by any means imply any renunciation of them on the part of the Church. This, I repeat, never happened; and if ecclesiastical authorities, in times of an innovating boldness of teaching, did allow the reins to pass too much from their hands, and occasionally permitted the liberty conceded to their teachers to be unworthily abused, still this was only a transient although great error of ecclesiastical jurisdiction. But the Church never abandoned aught of its rights, nor does their conduct establish any absurdity in the fundamental principles of the Protestant Churches. Would it be a fair and just inference, if from the cases in the English Episcopal Church in which unprincipled Clergy were for years continued in their functions to the spiritual detriment of their Cure, one were to attribute to the Church the disgraceful inconsistency, that, while she appointed the Clergy for the edification of their charge, she at the same time permitted them to give offence by their unchristian life? If Mr. R. will not allow this, but ascribes it to the deficiencies of individual spiritual authorities, how can he charge the Protestant Churches in Germany with inconsistency?

Closely connected with this confusion of the errors in the Functionaries with the principles of the Church, is the too great value which Mr. R. attaches to the preventive means for those evils which he observed in Germany. The English Episcopal Church may glory and rejoice in the character of her XXXIX Articles, she may from her point of view give them the preference over those longer formulæ, which had their origin in historical struggles and in the living Christian faith of their composers, (though I must repeat, that it is not in the nature of these confessions that the source of the weakness of the Authorities is to be sought;) she may think it right to bind her ministers by subscription to these Articles; nothing of all this do we wish to depreciate; still one cannot grant to its advocates that the disorders observed in Germany evidenced the necessity of laying " some check and restraint upon the human mind," nor that the binding force, the necessity of the subscription, the setting the letter of the symbol on the same level with its scriptural contents, can be regarded as the *source of the spiritual blessing* which the Church enjoys. The former would too much resemble the control which the Romish Church exerts over her members; the latter appears to involve too strange a confusion of the prevention of an evil with the existence of a good.

The necessity of deterring the ministers of a Church from the arbitrary aberrations of heresy, by binding them to human Articles, and of thereby assuming the right to remove them when convicted of erroneous doctrines, may often, perhaps always, exist; yet where it does exist, it presupposes an inclination to these heretical aberrations, and that in a degree proportionate to the apparent urgency of this necessity.

Such an inclination, however, in a considerable part of the Clergy, is no healthy condition, nor one productive of blessing. Its suppression is but the prevention of a yet greater evil than actually exists within the system. The blessing, however, the blessing of doctrines delivered by enlightened and believing men, must be derived elsewhere; from the spirit, namely, of grace and of prayer, which human forms can never give, but which they may by an unreasonable strictness hinder, though they cannot quench. When a Church then so far confides that this spirit of grace and of truth, which is the Spirit of Christ, will illumine her teachers, if duly prepared and called, as to trust that such unscriptural heretical aberrations, by which the basis of Christianity is shaken, should be but of rare occurrence; she may, indeed, go too far in this originally noble confidence, and may find herself compelled by experience to return more decisively to the preventive means and rules comprised in the documents upon which she was founded: in no event, however, will she be tempted to look for blessing and prosperity, from the establishment of the most definite verbal forms, from the erection of symbols independent of immediate controversy, and from a mode of restraint which places the human form of the doctrine on an equality with the word of Scripture. Had she such expectations, it were evident that she trusted more in the human formula than in the Spirit of Christ. While she trusts in this, she will indeed not neglect those means of protection; still she will make it her first aim to impart to her young Clergy, by a genuine theological preparation, that spirit which preaches the same Gospel under forms, varying indeed, yet all within the limits of the word of Scripture, and which produces adherence to, and justification of, the doctrine not after the letter but after the spirit of the symbol: for ill were the state of any ecclesiastical authorities who should be unable to discern and to exhibit this spirit; and lamentable the condition of any Church, which, besides the legal fences against error, did not believe in a source from which the truth issues in such a living stream, that error itself must progressively diminish, the administration of the law become continually more enlightened, the means of repression less and less necessary. Such belief, however, and such endeavours form the principles upon which the Evangelical Churches of Germany acted. If they stumbled occasionally in this noble course is that a sign they can never reach the object they proposed? and if their principles are grounded on faith in the Spirit of Christ, should they abandon them in the midst of their career, and recur to those which centre on a reliance upon the letter of the human form, and upon the restraining force of the law?

But this leads further to those other charges of Mr. R.'s work, which indeed constitute by far the most important portion of its contents, the condemnatory representation of the direction which theology took for so long a period, and in part still takes, in so great a portion of the German authors: and here it is my duty both candidly to avow the pain which I also feel at such numerous aberrations from the purity of Christian truth; and yet distinctly to indicate that this evil, when contemplated in the due connection with the free developement of theological science, (and how can science exist without freedom) appears partly to have taken place beyond the limits of the Church, partly to have been a necessary point of transition to a purer theology, partly to have been less widely extended than the author represents.

It is not necessary for us, my dear friend, to settle as a preliminary, whether those rationalist tendencies, through which the external and internal facts of Christianity are to be transmuted and solved into speculation and reflection, are disastrous and pernicious in any literature, and in any times.

Christianity is a divine fact, whose divine character, externally manifested, is inseparably united with an internal transformation of mind, which remains eternally distinct from any thing which man by his own device can produce: and yet will the rationalism of all times and all descriptions remove this distinction; this is its error, this its $\pi\rho\tilde{\omega}\tau ον$ $\psi ε\tilde{υ}\delta ος$, and herein is it at all times equally destructive, whether it employ itself in the sublimest speculations on the ideas contained in the facts of Christianity, or whether on the shallowest department of the common-place, empiric, factitious view of history it strain to evaporate the miracles of the sacred relation.

Yet must we confess that this rationalism appears from time to time in every people and every literature. England has felt its full presumption and full perniciousness, in its deism. In France it united itself, though not at all times entirely, with materialism: and in Germany, it appeared in the form of a baseless innovating interpretation of Scripture, a shallow, would-be enlightening philosophy of religion.

If then the author rightly says, that the distinctive and specially revolting characteristic of the German rationalism consists in its having made its appearance within the Church, and in the guise of Theology; this indeed cannot be denied, yet it is not true to the extent to which the author represents it. Many of those writers whom he quotes for their unscriptural positions and opinions, as Reimarus, Becker, Buchholz, &c., were never in any ecclesiastical or theological office: they wrote as men pursuing in entire independence their philosophical systems; and if the influence of some of them widely extended itself even among the theologians, yet are not their opinions upon that account to be charged upon the theology and the Church. Or can this be done with greater fairness, than if the deistical principles of a Hume and a Gibbon, nay of a Toland and Tindal, were to be imputed to the English theology? We may further take into consideration, that many of those scientific men, who went furthest in a superficial and forced interpretation of the sacred documents, belonged to the philosophical faculties in our universities: in these it has ever been a principle to allow science to speak out entirely unrestrained, even in opposition to the doctrine of the Church, in the confidence that the theological faculty, through greater depth, or the greater correctness of its point of view, would be able to supply a counterpoise: if we take this also into the account, no small portion of the blame is already removed from the theologians and the Church of Germany: the evil itself remains, but it appears more as connected with the philosophical and literary spirit of the time, than as a charge against the theology, which however it may have come in contact with, and been affected by, the philosophical endeavours of the age, has yet its own independent history; nor are the several portions of this so indistinct and confused as would appear from the notes of Mr. Rose.

And this constitutes the second point which I would

notice, namely, that not only in Mr. Rose's citations, but in the sketch given in the discourses themselves, the distinction of the different times and periods has been to so great a degree neglected: an omission, which has entirely obscured the several points of transition by which theology progressively advanced towards a purer and sounder state. How can your countrymen form a correct image of our literature, when Lessing and Schelling, Steinbart and Bretschneider, Töllner and Schleiermacher, Bahrdt and Wegscheider, Herder, and the anonymous author of the Vindiciæ sacræ N. T. scriptur., are mentioned together, without any other distinction than the often incorrect dates? Most of these authors who are thus named together, were separated by 30 or 40 years from each other; they may to the letter say the same thing, and yet the meaning in which they say it, and the influence which it has upon the times, are by no means the same; the earlier have, perhaps, suggested as an experiment what has long since been discarded; or they have started that as philosophers, which only the more superficial writers have attempted to convert into theology: several of them moreover had grown up in close connection with a period in which it was a duty to contend against a false orthodoxism which clung to the letter alone: while many of the weaker moderns have proceeded to develope their opinions into positions, against which those nobler strugglers for truth would themselves with great earnestness have contended. The neglect of these historical relations however, (which is not made good by the description of Semler) casts a false light upon the whole view. Had our author possessed a vivid conception of the spirit of German theology, which toward the middle of the preceding century was more rigidly attached, than was ever the case in England, to a false system of doctrine, combined with a confined idea of inspiration, and a stiff intolerant method of demonstration, which impeded the healthy process of a scriptural and deeper theology; had he moreover by the study of the noblest authors of our nation in that earlier period, whether in philosophy, or in practical or elegant literature, learnt the inward desire after a noble genuine freedom of mind, for which at that time Protestant and Romanist longed, he would deem the rise of a new and partly daring direction of theology, not only a natural but an interesting phenomenon; he would have acknowledged that in part the legitimate requisitions of science in philology and history, led to the adoption of that new course; that many also of those so-called innovators, were well conscious that they possessed a Christian and good scriptural foundation and object, but that almost all were so deficient in firm scientific principles in the execution of these views, that too much freedom and too open a course was given to the bad, the capricious, and the irreligious, to violate the sanctuaries of the Bible, by a semi-philosophical babbling and a lawless criticism.

If then this point of view be adhered to, that all German innovations in theology discharged themselves principally in two main channels; the one in which scientific clearness and freedom were the object of honest exertion, the other in which an inward indisposition toward the peculiar character of the Christian Religion, moulded the yet uncompleted results of historical investigation with a shallow philosophy into an unconnected revolting commixture of naturalism and popular philosophy, all the phenomena in the history of theology will be sufficiently explained. That better race of authors, for the most part too little acquainted with the principles of the science of scriptural interpretation, and the defence of religion, committed indeed many an error, but with a chastened judgment they again struck back into the right path. It was natural that they should occasionally fail at first sight to recognise the shallowness and pervertedness of enquiries of the second sort; and that to a certain degree participating in the fascination with which the spirit of that time had invested every species of tolerance, they should expose themselves to the injustice, by which their purer endeavours were subsequently confounded with those of the deistic naturalist;—an injustice frequently practised in these times in a crying manner, not by Romanists only, but by Protestants of too exclusive a system of theology. And now that this better sort of temperate, religiously disposed, and scientific enquirers have gained a better basis, rule, and method, partly through their own more enlarged acquaintance with the province of their science (to which belongs also the acknowledgment of its limits); partly through the exertions of decided apologists and apologetic doctrinal writers; partly, and not least, through the endeavours of a deeper philosophy; and lastly, in part through the religious stimulus caused by momentous political events; now also that studies in ecclesiastical history, alike deep in their character and pure in their point of view, have quickened the sight for discerning the essence of Christianity; our German theology is attaining a pure and scientific character, which it could not have acquired, so unfettered and in such full consciousness, without first discharging itself of those baser elements.

Much is yet left to be done, much to clear away; but the more that genuine apologetic and hermeneutic principles, derived from the nature of belief and of thought, possess themselves of the mind, the more will those falsifying theories of accommodation, those wretched explanations of miracles, those presumptuous critical hypotheses, give place to a perspicuous view of the essence of Divine Revelation, to a living understanding of the prophetic and apostolic writings, and consequently to a purer exposition of the main doctrines of Christianity. You must not allow this hope to be obscured by what you may have seen of the struggles of supernaturalism, and rationalism, or perhaps may read most obnoxiously exhibited in several of our periodical works. Within the province of proper theology this contest is not so important as it often appears, and the more it developes itself the less lasting can it be; inasmuch as an independent rationalism is irreconcileable with the very idea of Christian theology, and a bare supernaturalism, which goes no further than what its name expresses, does not contain the slightest portion of the substance and doctrines of Christianity. If then it is true, that through a genuine study of scriptural interpretation and of history, a better theology has begun to find place among us, the distracting influence which this conflict exerts, must of necessity here also be gradually diminished: on the other hand it will probably continue, possibly yet more develope itself, in the more direct province of religion, in philosophy and in politics, where amid many a struggle, and many an alternation, it may systematise itself in the contrast of a religious and of an atheistic, or of a sincere and of an hypocritical character of thought, and then again from the various points of mutual contact unavoidably re-act upon theology. This danger is, however, no other than that to which the English Episcopal, nay even the Romanist, and indeed every part of the Christian Church, is exposed; and this disease, thus universal to mankind, may indeed delay, but cannot preclude, the restoration of German theology, derived from the genuine sources of philological and historical investigation combined with that experience in faith, which brings the mind and heart in vivid contact with them.

If, however, Mr. Rose has failed to perceive the necessary course of developement of German theology, so neither has he become sufficiently acquainted with, nor duly appreciated, the counter workings, by which the further progress of the evil was even in the worst and most perplexed times opposed and checked. He names indeed Storr as an opponent of the rationalist school, yet so that no one could thence perceive that this theologian was only the representative of a party at all times considerable and important. He names the philosophy of Schelling, yet almost as if all the impulses in Religion and in the Church, which, for almost twenty years, have been tending to improvement and increased unity, were derived from the suspicious source of mystical philosophemata. Neither was the case. Storr was but the disciple of the whole school of Würtemberg and Tübingen, of which he was subsequently the head; a school which, without being exempt from the errors of the time, has now for between thirty and forty years united in its writings the most conscientious earnestness with the deepest investigation. Here should have been mentioned together with Storr the names and the works of the two Flatts, of Süsskind, Bengel, Steudel, &c. To the same effect notice should also have been taken of Reinhard, who, chiefly by the pure means of works alike classical and theological, promoted an improved spirit in Saxony; of Knapp, who, but lately deceased, blended the purest orthodoxy with classical attainments, which might satisfy even English scholars, and with a depth of scriptural interpretation, which was the object of respect in every school; of Hess, the venerable investigator and relator of biblical history; of the works of Planck on Theological Encyclopædia, and in defence of Christianity; of Kleuker in Kiel, Schott in Jena, Schwarz in Heidelberg, and of the direction (in part one of scientific depth) decisively opposed to the common rationalism, which the theological faculty of Berlin has by its historical and philosophical investigations, for more than fifteen years imparted to theological study. All this must be viewed in connection with the great number of well-disposed and Christian practical Clergy in evangelical Germany, and with the almost universal removal of the lower classes from unchristian books upon religion. It should have been acknowledged, that in certain parts of Germany and Switzerland, Christian societies existed for the purpose of mutually imparting biblical and Christian knowledge, and for the circulation of the Scriptures, even previous to the (it must be confessed, somewhat too vehement) impulse given by the British Bible Society. It should have been noticed, how the community of the

Moravian brethren exerted, upon the whole, a very deep and gentle influence (even though not altogether exempt from error) upon the very highest as well as upon the lowest classes, in producing the reception of the fundamental doctrines of Christianity, especially of the Atonement. It should have been remarked, that the entirely voluntary associations in Bible and Missionary Societies could not have been so universal and so great, as is upon the whole the case, without a considerable foundation of Christian disposition; this and so much more therewith connected, must be more accurately known, investigated deeper, and exhibited in more connexion, before the theology and Church of Protestant Germany can be displayed in their real form; and they would then certainly not appear so revolting and so offending as they are represented in Mr. R.'s work.

Should these remarks have now made it clear that the foundations upon which the theology of Protestant Germany may be raised to a high degree of pure Christian and scientific elevation, are, through the blessing of God, already laid on the deep basis of her improved principles, neither can one share the great expectations which the author entertains from the introduction among ourselves of fixed liturgies, and an ecclesiastical constitution resembling that of the Episcopal Church. Be it here undecided how far the one or the other could in themselves contribute to a better state of things; thus much at least is certain, that in a church accustomed, in the noblest sense of the word, to so much freedom as that of Evangelical Germany, and which, without any external interference, is at this moment conscious of a voluntary return to the fundamental evangelical principles, (a return in which all its earlier spiritual and scientific advances are comprised and guaranteed,) political restraint can be neither necessary nor beneficial. Those, however, who conceive that they can observe in the theology and Church of Evangelical Germany an internal formative principle, tending to realize a high Christian purity, while they do not ascribe the same value as the author to the measure which he proposes, will attach themselves so much the more firmly to one, which they regard as proceeding from the same principle, and of which the author speaks with an almost inconceivable suspicion. You will perceive, that I speak of the union of the Lutheran and Reformed Churches in Germany; and I must confess to you, that it is the judgment passed upon this, which appears to me to fix the stamp of misconception upon every thing else which is unclear in the work. Had the author but recalled to mind, that in the period of the greatest indifference to religion and church, the division of these two parties continued unregarded and unmitigated; that the endeavour to remove it coincided with the renewal of a warm interest in divine worship and in the Church, had he allowed himself to be informed, that it originated with men very far removed from indifferentism, and promoted by that very evangelically-disposed king of Prussia, from whom he himself anticipates so much, he could scarcely have ascribed the union to motives so bad. But had he (which he at all events both could and ought) informed himself, that the one difference in doctrine between the two Churches is of such a nature, that the distinction can scarcely be retained in the symbolical books of the Church even by a straw-splitting nicety, (this is the case with regard to the doctrine of the Lord's Supper in the two Churches) while the other, that regarding election, never existed in Germany, (in that the strict Calvinistic doctrine is not at all expressed in the symbol of the German reformed Church, the Heidelberg Catechism) and that Brandenburg expressly refused to acknowledge the definitions of the synod of Dort respecting it; had he weighed this he would have spared himself this hostility against a work, in its nature originating in Christian brotherly love, and which has already produced in many countries, especially in Prussia and Baden, the cheering fruits of reanimated interest in the Church.

Yet enough; for you, my worthy friend, I have made

myself sufficiently intelligible, and should I, through your means, perhaps, contribute to prepare a portion of your countrymen for a correcter view of the character of Protestant Germany, I should deem myself happy in thereby repaying a small portion of the debt, which the privilege of surveying the character of your English Church, in its important and pure (though as yet unreconciled) contrasts, has laid upon me. And if I might express a wish, which forces itself upon me at the close of this long letter, it is, that more of your young theologians would visit our Protestant Universities, become acquainted with our theologians, and hear our preachers, only not making a transient and hasty stay, nor living principally amid books, but acquainting themselves with the people, and the Church, and the literature, in their real character, and ready for mutual confidential interchange of their different talents.

With real regard and esteem,

Your's most sincerely,

CHARLES HENRY SACK,

Professor of Theology, and Minister of the Evangelical Church of Bonn.

BONN,
July 27, 1827.

HISTORICAL ENQUIRY,

&c.

HUMAN nature, as in itself it for the most part remains the same, so does it continue upon the whole in the same relation to Christianity, opposes the same obstacles to its first reception, and to the complete exertion of its influence, furnishes the same temptations to substitute for it a mere passive acquiescence in its doctrines, or to convert it into a mere material for the speculation of the understanding. Still more uniform than the existence of the obstacles themselves is the natural tendency of each aberration to re-produce another, for the most part its opposite, extreme. The form, however, of the impediments, and the prominence assumed by each, will be in great measure modified and determined by the degree of civilization, by the peculiarities and predominant tendency of each age, by national character, and by national circumstances. Fruitful then as must be every portion of ecclesiastical history, in exhibiting the inherent power of Christianity to conquer the different difficulties to which it is opposed, in proving it to be the leaven, by which the whole mass of human nature is to be penetrated and changed, and in supplying the knowledge of the conditions by which the full exertion of that influence is limited; more especially productive must those portions be, which relate to its struggles in nations, derived from the same common stock, under circumstances in many respects similar, and above all, where the remedy applied was equally freed from the grossest of those extraneous admixtures, which in other less favoured countries create a prejudice against its use, or diminish its efficacy. The experience furnished by Evangelical Germany is to us as the biography of an individual to one of similar character, temperament, and circumstances. The plant, though its growth and external character may be affected by the influence of a different climate, will not belie its original stock : nor can the atmosphere of a neighbouring region be changed, without the probability of its affecting our own. Linked as European nations are, every direction which the human character takes in one country must exert an influence over the rest; the circulation may be rendered more or less rapid by the peculiar subordinate organization of each ; yet still is the whole one great system, no part of which can be affected without indirectly operating upon the rest, in a degree proportioned to the general analogies of their constitution. Nor is it nationally alone that the result of German experience may benefit ourselves; the moral and religious history of mankind is but an enlarged biography; should therefore no crisis be impending over this country, similar to that from which Germany is now recovering, (and, with some similarities, there is still sufficient which is dissimilar, to justify the hope that we shall be preserved from such a visitation,) much individual profit and warning may be obtained from the study. The several, and not unfrequently opposite, aberrations which took place in Germany, and which terminated in the temporary unbelief of so large a portion of its speculating minds, has not unfrequently been realized in the deflection of a single individual. Independently, moreover, of its personal as well as national utility, it affords in itself a sublime contemplation of the innate force of pure Christianity, which, instead of sinking irrevocably, as the falling stars of the false religions of old, or the now waning crescent of Mohammedanism, shines forth again with a clearer brightness, and a more vivifying warmth, from amid the clouds which were for awhile permitted to obscure its face. Superstitions or false belief, foundations of "wood, hay, stubble [1]," when tried by the fire, disappear for ever; divine truth, as the "silver and gold," in each successive trial to which it has been exposed, has come forth purer from the human alloy which had collected round it.

A large, however, and extensive survey will be necessary, whenever this crisis is to be fully understood. Completely comprehended, indeed, it can then only be, when time shall have more entirely disclosed the results, to which Providence

---

[1] 1 Cor. iii. 12.

has through this fearful developement been conducting the Evangelical Church in Germany; though enough may be already seen to lay open His general purposes, and to furnish comfort amid that temporary desolation in the gladdening results of a purer, more active, more vivifying faith, which are even now apparent. Even the causes, however, by which these events were immediately produced, can only be fully discovered by a wide and accurate study of the previous history, from a period long prior to their commencement. No revolution or developement in the moral, or political, any more than in the physical world, can be understood from the single contemplation of the times alone in which it takes place. The producing causes must evidently be anterior to the commencement of the manifestation of the results. As in vegetable nature, the seed has long been prepared, the root has already struck, before the first indications of the germ above the surface, so, for the most part, has the train of producing causes been long imperceptibly in action, before they give any visible manifestations of their agency; the developement itself is almost inevitable, before the tendency of circumstances to produce it is generally felt. But if such is the case in civil, much more is it in religious, history, since this exhibits not the result of irregular, undefined, and often jarring, principles; but the application of one uniform system, the course of one great plan for the elevation, purifying, hallowing, of the human mind, in the vast contest, which in the words of one of the most philosophic observers of Germany, forms the only and the deepest theme of the history of the world and of man, the contest of faith and unbelief[1]. An unity thus necessarily belongs to ecclesiastical history, which no other history, even of principles, at least to the same degree, can claim; and the necessity of considering each given period in combination with the whole, or at all events with a large preceding portion, becomes manifestly more indispensable. Throughout this vast course, however, there occurs a series of elevations, from which the survey of the several intervening stages is facilitated, and the relation of the whole scheme to each tendency of the human mind, which it is given to correct, becomes more distinct. Uniform as this scheme is in itself, the subordinate principles, with which it is brought in contact in successive ages, will necessarily vary: and as, in combination or in conflict with these, it either proceeds tranquilly onward, modifying and being in its external character modified by them, or, having reached a crisis, manifests itself more energetically in the new developement to which this crisis gives rise, there have been and will be a succession of periods and of eras in its history. Each new era is the commencement of a new period, in which the results of the former crisis are carried on in gradual progress; each new period prepares for a new crisis, as soon as the human principles, with which Christianity has been brought

[1] Göthe Westöstlicher Divan, S. 224.

in contact, or by which it has been acted upon, shall have acquired sufficient strength to induce a re-action, if the foreign ingredients be combined with it; a collision, if they be opposed. Each period then will be best understood from the preceding crisis or era; each era requires for its explanation the knowledge of the preceding period. In the periods also, or at least in their later portions, it appears, Christianity will be most mingled with, or opposed by, extraneous principles; in the eras, it will most exert its native and original powers. The last great crisis in the Christian Church in Germany preceding that, which is now being developed, was the Reformation; and from that time, therefore, must any full investigation of the course of things, which led to the present, commence. This, however, though upon the whole one period, in that no complete crisis intervened in it, can be subdivided, accordingly as the system, which became predominant, was either pre-eminently engaged in the process of formation, or in maintaining itself against its various antagonists. It must, however, be kept in view, that this division is subordinate; inasmuch as these conflicts, till the final collision with unbelief, succeeded indeed in detaching portions from the sway of that system, but not in modifying its character. Within the limits, which it yet retained, its developement continued, until the final crisis by which it was overthrown. It will be further necessary in any complete view, to consider distinctly the two elements of Theology, the religious basis and the scientific form; though mutually acting upon each other, it is only by a distinct consideration, that the very different efforts, which in the close of this period tended to the same results, can be understood and appreciated. The minor periods then are, I.—The formation of the system from the Reformation, and its developement through the Formula of Concord until the first opposition. II.—The Opposition, 1. on the scientific side by Calixtus, 2. on the religious side by Spener and the school of Halle carrying on the earlier efforts of Arndt, 3. both on its scientific and religious side, either by the partial but honest endeavours of men, whose sole object was to remove its errors, or by unbelief in its various gradations.

Much, both in the external and internal circumstances of the German Reformation, occurred to prevent its full and adequate developement. Had this been perfected in the spirit in which its great instrument might have completed it, if permitted tranquilly to finish his work, or supported by others, acting in his own principles, and surveying the whole system of Revelation with the comprehensive and discriminating view of his master-mind, the history of the German Church had probably been altogether different; the results, which it is now reaching after centuries, and at which it is arriving through such a fearful transition, might have been even then attained. A great part of the really valuable principles, which have resulted from the late collisions, may be found, unsystematized indeed, occasionally only implied, in the works of Luther. The fruitless attempts to satisfy an uneasy and active conscience by the meritorious performances of a Romish convent had opened his eyes to the right understanding of Scripture, in whose doctrines alone it could find rest; and the clear and discerning faith which this correspondence of Scripture with his own experience strengthened in him, gave him that intuitive insight into the nature of Christianity, which enabled him for the most part unfailingly to discriminate between essentials and non-essentials, and raised him not only above the assumed authority of the church, and above the might of tradition, but above the influence of hereditary scholastic opinions, the power of prejudices, and the dominion of the letter. Unfortunately, however, the further expansion of his views necessarily yielded to the then yet more important practical employments, to which this great apostle of evangelical truth dedicated the most of his exertions;—the instruction of the young, the care of all the churches, the necessary struggles with the Romish Church, or with those seceders from it, who maintained tenets inconsistent with the first principles of the Reformation, as in the opposed errors of the Anabaptists, and of Zwingli. His successors, in developing to the utmost subordinate but contested points of his system, neglected the great views which lay beyond the sphere of their polemics. Few, comparatively, in the large mass of the active agents in the

Reformation, were led to the rejection of the errors of the Church of Rome through the same school of experience, by which the master-mover had been conducted. Many had been merely theoretically convinced of its errors, others sought a freedom from intellectual tyranny, others political advantages, some finally followed, but half consciously, the mighty impulse. The number of the noble band, who were actuated by the same spirit which impelled Luther, was diminished, and their agency disturbed by the troubles of the times; by which e. g. Melanchthon and Chytræus became for some time wanderers in Germany; Bucer acquired among ourselves a new scene of evangelical exertion. More fatal than the impediments thus presented to the tranquil developement of the principles of the Reformation were the internal divisions, originating in an imperfect conception of its scheme, which distracted its members, and diverted their attention from its essential points to subjects of very subordinate importance, or upon which controversy should never have been raised. These had been checked indeed by the commanding spirit of Luther; after his death (1546) no one was left of sufficient authority or firmness to prevent their eruption, or to lead back the current. Even in Melanchthon's life, the Adiaphoristic[1]

---

[1] Henke infers from this controversy being confined to the Electorate of Saxony, exclusive of Brandenburg, where the obnoxious compliances were carried to a greater extent, that not the supposed errors, but the school of Melanchthon, was the real object of attack. (Kirchengesch. iii. 418.)

controversy, (a controversy, which, from the neglect of the simple but comprehensive principles of St. Paul, has, under different forms in various ages, been destructive of Christian charity, and drawn down the minds of Christians to minute and subordinate questions from the great and influential truths of the Gospel,) the Majoristic [1], Synergistic [2], Flacianist [3], Osiandrist [4], Stanca-

---

[1] Major's doctrine of the necessity of good works to salvation, had appeared without offence in Melanchthon's loci Theol. 1535, as well as in the translation by Justus Jonas, 1536. Being however repeated in the Interim of Leipzig, in which Major had a share, it served to swell the papistical errors which were to be found in it. Major throughout maintained justification by faith alone, willingly pledged himself not to use the offensive expression, yet was compelled publicly to recant. One of his principal antagonists, as is known, held " that they were hurtful to salvation." Schröckh Kircheng. B. 39, S. 548, fgg.

[2] The doctrine questioned had appeared with Luther's approbation in Melanchthon's Examen ordinandorum in the scholastic form, that there were three causes of conversion, God, God's Word, and Free-will, (Vater. K. G. 225.) implying, however, (according to Pfeffinger's explanation in the present contest) " that though the human will could not awaken or rouse itself " to good works, but must be awakened by the Holy Spirit, yet " that man was not altogether excluded from such works of the " Holy Spirit, to the degree that he should not also do his share." (Planck Gesch. des Prot. Lehrbegr. ap. Schr. ib. 554.)

[3] The principal subject of the controversies in which Flacius was, on the defensive, engaged, was an assertion made in the vehemence of his opposition to Strigel, that " original sin was the substance of human nature."

[4] Brentius, who wrote as the organ of the theologists of Würtemberg, concluded their judgment by saying, that if the theologians of Königsberg would interpret each other's words in Christian love, and not explain unusual or imperfect expressions with the greatest rigour and in the worst sense, they would not then

rian [1], had unceasingly torn the infant church [2]; nor can it have been the mere love of peace, but rather the deep and oppressive sense of the impediments presented to the progress of the truth by these endless and by him incurable dissentions, which made Melanchthon gladly hail approaching death as a refuge from the phrenzy (rabie) of the Theologians [3]; nor was it merely as his own anxious wish, but rather as the most important principle

contend against each other as against Turks, especially as this dispute could produce no useful result. (ap. Schr. ib. 579.) Though the whole question was whether δικαιωθῆναι signified " to be acquitted," as Osiander held, or to be made righteous, and whether, (it being allowed on both sides, that our righteousness was derived from the perfect obedience of Christ, and his obedience resulting from his divine nature) Christ were our righteousness solely according to his divine nature, Osiander was accused by a synod of " destroying the whole merit of the atonement of Christ." (Schröckh, ib. 582.) The people were warned in sermons against his devilish heresy, (ib. 578.) and the command of Duke Albrecht of Prussia to wave the contested point in their sermons, declared by his opponents to have emanated from the devil. (Ib. 581.)

[1] The over-speculation of Osiander naturally produced the reaction, that the work of justification was ascribed by Stancarus to the human nature alone of Christ.

[2] Schlüsselberg, who has more fully than any other contemporary writer enumerated the contests of his times, composed his " Catalogus Hereticorum," in 13 8vo. volumes, describing as many classes of deviations. (Schr. ib. 484.)

[3] Melch. Adam. Vita Germ. Philos. p. 93. That these evils, not the depreciation and revilings of his own name and character, were what Melanchthon principally felt, see in Heerbrand Pr. Funebr. in ob. Mel. in Strobel's Miscell. St. vi. S. 215. Strobel's Apologia Mel. wider Göze.

which he could impress upon his times, that he wrote as his motto and memorial in the alba of his contemporaries, " a contentioso Theologo libera nos, bone Deus." Far be it from us, however, who are removed by the differences of age and manners from the temptations to which these often well-intentioned men were exposed, who, though our faith be equally the result of independent conviction, have yet had the easier task of examining an existing system by the test of Scripture, instead of that of constructing it for ourselves from the ruins of one deformed by human additions, and whom the lapse of time has for the most part enabled to discriminate between the vital and the subordinate truths of the Gospel, to judge harshly of those, whose difficulties we have not experienced. It was, perhaps, natural, certainly pardonable, that accustomed by early and deeply impressed habit, in the Church which they had left, to attach an equal value to every doctrine, and dazzled by the adscititious interest, with which the recency and difficulty of the acquisition had invested every portion of the newly obtained truths, they failed to appreciate the relative value of those truths; especially as these were, for the most part, opposed to a system, every portion of which was inculcated as of equal importance, every departure from which was represented as an equal sin: it was natural also, that those who differed in opinion should be suspected of disaffection to the common cause; and consequently, that as every error seemed to be an error in essentials, those should appear the least excuseable, who in other points approached the nearest to the truth, and in whom, therefore, from the general correctness of their views, a single aberration would appear the result of wilfulness. These principles would of course exert a similar influence upon the human deductions or speculations by which they fenced, or defined, the newly-acquired divine truths. External circumstances, however, also contributed to foster this uncompromising refusal to allow of the slightest deviation, even in the minuter and collateral points, which had once been sanctioned. The unhappy limitation of the toleration, guaranteed by the religious peace of Augsburg, to the adherents of the Augsburg Confession, and the undisguised anxiety of the Romanists to take advantage of any deviation from the letter of that Confession [1], to ex-

[1] Many of these attacks, either upon the validity of a religious peace generally, or upon its extension to those who only accepted the Confession with Melanchthon's later alteration, are related in Salig's Vollständ. Hist. der Augsb. Conf. Th. 1. S. 772. fg.; see also Budd. Isag. 429. 441. Among these one of the most remarkable was written by the private secretary of the Emperor, 1586 (Schröckh Kirchengesch. B. 39. S. 338. fg.) It is well known that the Reformed were not formally included in the religious peace until nearly a century afterwards, by the peace of Westphalia; that even then this acknowledgment was protested against by the Elector of Saxony, and obtained only by the asseveration of the Elector of Brandenburg, that he accepted every thing which was verbally contained in the confession of Augsburg, and by the interposition of Holland and Sweden; even then the theological distinction was maintained by the substitution of the words "inter illos," for "inter hos," which latter would have directly

clude them from the protection which it afforded bound them to its letter, as the safeguard of their privileges or their existence. The common-place and shallow argument also, drawn from the variations of the evangelical statements of doctrine against the truth of their system itself, which was even then urged, was met not by the easy task of retort upon the Romish Church, nor by the obvious principle that all human discoveries of truth must be gradual, must be effected by the slow and toilsome passage through error, nor by shewing that these discrepancies in collateral points, or modes of statement, were still entirely consistent with the truth and harmony of the general system, but by drawing still closer the limits of their Churches' pale, and by excluding as heretics all who departed from the strictest letter of the symbol. The Protestant princes, who had embraced the Reformation rather from feeling than from clear views, felt themselves responsible for the doctrines of their clergy; and, perplexed by the differences of the Socinians, Anabaptists, Fanatics, and their own controversialists, sought to obviate discordance by minute and detailed con-

---

included them among the members of the Augsburg Confession, (see authorities in Schröckh, ib. 347; Henke, K. G. B. 3. S. 596 fg.; Vater, K. G. S. 269.) Even after this the theologians of Wittenberg taught, that this, as a political measure, could not affect the theological question, (Henke, B. 4. S. 272.) After this time, however, the political interests of the two evangelical bodies, in that the voices of both together only equalled those of the one Romanist, became identified.

fessions: in other cases their political jealousies, especially those of the two lines of the house of Saxony, of which the younger had dispossessed the elder of the Electorate (1547), aided to give bitterness to these contests[1]. Not theologians merely, but jurists, historians, even physicians, participated in the acrimony of the elder branch[2]. Yet, however these and other difficulties may prevent our assuming an uncharitable right to condemn the successors of the Reformers, certain it is, that the measures employed to produce uniformity, miserably impeded the progress of the Reformation, buried in great measure the hardly won evangelical truth under a load of scholastic definitions, and converted the Gospel truth itself, when it shone dimly through, into matter of speculation, instead of motive for practice. The history of Christian controversy scarcely exhibits more unhappy, more unpractical, and frequently presumptuous polemics, than many of those which distracted the German Church after the death of Luther, unless perhaps in the eastern controversies[3] on the person of the Redeemer,

---

[1] Schröckh, ib. 554. In these originated the foundation of the University of Jena, as a bulwark of genuine Lutheranism against the falsifications of the then Melanchthonian Wittenberg: the new edition of Luther's works, in opposition to the alleged corruptions of the collection of Wittenberg, was a proof of the spirit in which it was founded, as also the strictest and most polemical Lutherans, such as Flacius, were invited thither.

[2] Henke, 3. 411. fgg.

[3] The Annals of Eutychius furnish, perhaps, the fullest proof

or the endless straw-splittings of the schoolmen. Little, indeed, could be hoped from measures so little in unison with the principles of the Reformation, as the attempt to re-establish a minute uniformity by the oppressive accumulation of new formulæ of faith, or by the infliction of civil, sometimes the severest, penalties for minute declensions even from the human system. Both, however, were extensively employed. Of the latter it may be sufficient to mention the imprisonment of Strigel[1], the deposition and banishment of Hardenberg[2], (1561), the ten years confinement of the physician Peucer[3], and the death

that the uncharitableness of controversy is in proportion to its unpracticalness. See Annales Eutych. ed. Pococke, Oxon.

[1] To obtain Strigel's release, after he had been confined three years for maintaining, that man was not merely passive in the work of his conversion, not evangelical princes only, but the catholic Maximilian interfered. Schröckh, ib. 560.

[2] Hardenberg, minister in Bremen, was banished from the whole of Lower Saxony, for approximating to the reformed doctrine on the communion, though he admitted a sacramental distribution of the body of Christ, distinct from the participation by the faithful, (Schröckh, ib. 602) that the body of Christ was distributed with, but not in, the bread. (ib. 600.) His followers were deposed, and excluded from the communion. In the course of the proceedings an edict of 1534 is referred to, which directed the immediate expulsion of Anabaptists and Sacramentarists from Bremen. The persecutors of Hardenberg, having afterwards willingly resigned their offices rather than cease from revilings in the pulpit, succeeded in inducing Hamburg and Lubeck to exclude Bremen from their league, and renounce her commerce, as a protectress of heresies. Her trade suffered also, from the same cause, in Dantzig, and other places.

[3] Peucer's offence was the recommending for the theological

of Cracau, a Jurist, in consequence of torture, with the banishment or imprisonment of the other Crypto-Calvinists of Saxony (1574), measures re-enacted against the same party after a temporary encouragement (1591), with the additional blot of the death of Krell their chief after ten years confinement [1], (1601) and the deposition and banishment of Huber [2] for a mere variation in

chairs at Wittenberg zealous followers of Melanchthon, and the share which he had in promoting the reception of their catechism, which yet asserts, that in the receiving the Sacrament, the Son of God is truly, and *according to his substance*, present. (Schröckh, ib. 615.) The reason why Cracau was put to the torture is not known; yet he was apprehended as a promoter of the Philippian school. These two cases are the stronger, in that neither belonged to the theological body, and both were men of distinguished talents. Cracau had had a principal share in the " Constitutions of Augustus," the celebrated reform of Saxon law. (Schröckh, ib. 619.) Neither were the other depositions confined to theologians, (ib. 621.) another eminent man died after two years imprisonment. " Others," says Schröckh, " met with similar fates." (Ibid.)

[1] The final sentence against Krell, Chancellor of Christian I. of Saxony, imputed to him secret practices with foreign courts, (the supplying Henry IV. with troops against the league.) This, though the pretext, cannot have been the real reason, since four years expired before the nature of his accusation was agreed upon. It seems probable that the jealousy of the nobility, whom he had in great measure excluded from office, combined with his attempted innovations in religion, was the cause of his fate. (See Schröckh, ibid. 649—659.)

[2] Huber maintained that the Calvinistic predestination could only be effectually opposed by the assumption of an " universal election to eternal life;" yet this he so explained, that it became entirely equivalent to the " universal call, offer of mercy," &c. The contest was miserably prolonged by the obstinacy in adhe-

the mode of stating the Lutheran doctrine, that none are excluded from salvation. Depositions of all the clergy of a province, who refused to subscribe a newly introduced formula, were not unfrequent, where the prince passed from the Lutheran to the Reformed Church: yet here the intemperance [1] of the clergy often mitigated, often justified, the proceeding. The similar enactments of the Lutheran Church had no plea but the supposed necessity of a strict adherence to the letter of its founder. The effect of these violent measures was in their own nature transitory or partial; from the unsettled state of Germany, those expelled from one province were preferred in another. More efficacious in producing an at least external uniformity was the other measure of binding down the Protestant freedom by formulæ, more and more closely rivetted, until the human mind could take no step except in the leading-strings of authority. Of these formulæ, enacted for the most part for separate lands, the majority are known principally through the cata-

rence to terms, and by the invidious use of the names of former heretics (see Schröckh, ib. 661-5.)

[1] This is the more credible from the general vehemence of the Lutheran clergy. It is expressly mentioned by Schröckh in palliation. (Ib. 374, 5. 381, 2, &c.) Even within the Lutheran Church itself, we find the edict of Augustus, Elector of Saxony, forbidding all strife in the pulpit about the Adiaphorists, Majorists, and Synergists, regarded as an undue limitation of the pastoral office, and the Consistorium of Leipzig consulted whether such a command were unchristian. (Schr. ib. 612.) see also Henke, 3. 452.

logues in which they are enumerated[1]; they have perhaps an historical value, rather from the light which they cast upon the spirit of the times, than from any extensive influence which they exerted. More fatal, because more widely, and at last almost universally, received, was the formula of Concord. Until this was adopted, a certain latitude was still allowed by the symbolical books, though not indeed equal to that permitted by our own articles; notwithstanding some exceptions, still upon the whole, similarity of principle, rather than exact uniformity of expression, or of minute mode of conception, was made the condition of belonging to the Lutheran communion; some points were left altogether undefined; and the re-union of the Protestant churches, (which perhaps had never been divided had Calvin, instead of Zwingli, been the original founder of the Reformed, or might have speedily again been blended, had Luther survived[2], when the fair prospect died away through the timidity

[1] See Köcher Biblioth. Theol. Symbol. p. 114. Feuerlein Biblioth. Symb. Eccles. Luther. J. G. Walch Introd. in 1. Symbol. G. G. Meyer 1. Symb. util. et Hist. subscript. eorund. Gött. 1796. It may suffice to name the Confutation-book of Weimar (1558) against the Synergists, the Symbol formed at Stuttgard (1559) enforcing the doctrine of the ubiquity of Christ's body, (Schr. ib. 606.) and the Corpus Doctrinæ Pruthenicum against the Osiandrists. (1567.)

[2] Calixtus, whose accuracy is unquestioned, says that Luther became gradually more inclined to an union. (de Tolerantia Ref. ap. Schr. ib. 498.

of Melanchthon, and the vehemence of the ultra-Lutheran Westphal [1]) (1552) was still open, and might gradually have been effected by the mediation of the Crypto-Calvinists. The face of things was changed by the introduction of the formula of concord [2]. The moderate party of the Lutheran Church, which in accordance to Melanchthon's wise counsel confined itself to the Scriptural expressions on the communion, and which, though inferior, was still considerable [3], was annihilated, or passed into the Reformed Church; the desirable union of the two churches in Germany itself, was for above two centuries and a half delayed. The immediate object of the new formula was indeed so far effected, that the existing contests were laid aside; the scene of warfare, however, was changed, not peace produced [4]: struggles about the reception of the formula itself, about the altered and unaltered Augsburg Confession, and the contests with the reformed, succeeded; so that the only permanent fruits of this restriction were, on the one hand, the exclusion of many who in principle agreed

---

[1] Mosh. cent. xvi. iii. 2. c. 3. § 6.

[2] In its first form as the Articles of Torgau, (1574) though such that the theologians of Wittenberg signed it at last, after undergoing imprisonment, only with restrictions, even it was deemed too favorable to the Crypto-Calvinists. Budd. ib. 433.

[3] Schröckh, ibid. 623, 649.

[4] Mosheim, ibid. c. 1. § 40. sq. Henke, ibid. 457, fgg. Budd, ibid. 435, sq.

with the Lutheran doctrines; on the other, the enforcement of the letter [1] of the Lutheran tenets,

[1] It was a natural, though injurious, consequence of the great superiority of Luther, that every expression of his upon controverted points became a norm for the party, which, at all times the largest, was at last co-extensive with the Church itself. This almost idolatrous veneration was perhaps increased by the selection of declarations of faith, of which the substance on the whole was his, for the Symbolical books of his Church. At least, it is remarkable, that in the Reformed Churches, where the original articles were not taken from the works of the chief founder, no such scrupulous adherence to the expressions of that founder ever existed. On the other hand even in the earlier Lutheran controversies, the question is often, not whether the tenet agree with Scripture, but " whether it be a deflection from Luther's doctrine,"— " whether the individual be fallen away from Luther," whether " if the expression be the same, it be used precisely in the sense of Luther," (e. g. of Osiander, Vat. 5, 229. Schr. ib. 577. so also in the collateral definitions on the sacrament.) " Much as both parties were indebted to Luther, it is still strange to see the constant reference in the one, not merely to what Luther taught, but what expressions, what grounds, what ideas he had on collateral points; and this with the view of not varying a hair's-breadth from him." (ib. 599.) These principles were made universal by the formula of Concord; in this, ideas, which Luther had only thrown out in controversy, or had recalled, or which were at all events secondary only, became primary articles of faith; till this was received, even the then symbolical books were not exclusively adopted; they appear in different countries with different modifications; and it was yet doubtful whether the milder form in the Corpus Doctrinæ Christianæ Philippicum, and the Consensus Dresdensis, might not prevail. A greater freedom had occasionally been left; not only could Hardenberg declare, that on his appointment he had only bound himself to adhere to the Bible and the ancient Christian doctrine, (Schr. ib. 601.) but the synod of Hesse, in rejecting the formula of Concord, held the language, that it was not expedient that all the writings of

the establishment of mere scholastic opinions as articles of faith, the substitution of human technicalities for the free spirit of the Gospel, of a logical formalism for the scriptural and living expression of revealed truth. From the time that this formula was, through the influence of the Universities, generally received, and the ultra Lutheran compendium of Hutter [1] substituted there as

---

Luther, which were so unequal, should be thus extolled as rules of doctrine; that the Evangelical Church had already been reproached with submitting to a Babylonian captivity; that no man should be so much trusted to the detriment of conscience, &c. (Schr. ib. 627.) After the second attempt to approximate to the Reformed doctrine, the formula of Concord was in Saxony further guarded (1592) by a new temporary symbolical book, the Visitation-Articel, for not subscribing which, many distinguished men, and among them the celebrated Schindler, who first promoted the enlarged study of Hebrew, were deposed. (Schröckh ib. 660, 1. Budd. 440.)

[1] This was not only introduced into all the schools of Saxony to the exclusion of every other, but was to be learnt by heart with the greatest accuracy practicable before going to the university. The spirit of the author may be judged of from his other works, as the Calvinista aulico-politicus, in which he warns the clergy of Brandenburg against the accursed Calvinism; (Schröckh. ib. 385.) his loci Communes Theologici, whose object was to correct and replace the heresies of Melanchthon; and his Calvinus Judaizans, hoc est Judaicæ scholæ et corruptelæ, quibus J. Calvinus illustrissima S. S. loca et testimonia de gloriosissima Trinitate, Deitate Christi et Spiritus S.—detestandum in modum corrumpere non exhorruit." The ground of which charge was the greater discrimination, which Calvin employed in adducing evidence for the Trinity, and in admitting prophecies and types of Christ in the Old Testament. As a system of theology, the work of Hutter is not sufficiently connected, is unpractical, and meagre:

the basis of instruction for the loci theologici of Melanchthon, nothing remained but to proceed onward in the groove into which they had been forced to enter, to develope in still greater minuteness the fixed, immutable, definitions of the sanctioned form[1], to offer solutions of its difficulties, and to refute its opponents. It was to be expected from human nature, that party-spirit, thus fostered, should fail in none of its destructive effects. The circumstances of the age, as above observed, in themselves nurtured it; it had already painfully manifested itself in the vehement contentions within the Lutheran church, in the refusal to admit to the Lord's table, or to grant honourable burial to those, who on some minuter speculative points disagreed[2]. It did in fact in-

---

as a compendium, it is burthened with over-refined discussions; twenty pages being, for example, devoted to the developement of the doctrine of the union of the two natures in Christ, and the communicatio idiomatum. It continued, however, for a century to be one of the most favourite compendia; (Langemack Hist. Catechet. P. iii. p. 13.) that, which was its principal object, to combat the errors of the Romanists and the Reformed, remaining during that period the almost exclusive aim of doctrinal theology. The principal commentators upon it are mentioned by Budd. Isag. p. 351.

[1] Spener mentions that the symbolical books were often arbitrarily adduced in support of deductions, of which their authors never thought. (ap. Weism. 1227.)

[2] E. g. even laymen, who would not sign the confutation-book (against Synergism) were excluded from acting as sponsors, and even from honourable burial; (Henke 3. 420) so were the non-Flacianists; (Schr. ib. 571.) the Osiandrists by the opposed party of Mörlin, (Vater, S. 223.) and the students of Wittenberg

crease. The monuments of that age, whether theological works, or the public opinions of the universities, are but too deeply stamped with it; and agreeably to its genuine principles, the slightest approach to any tenet, or rite, or observance, of the opposed party, or the faintest disapprobation of any of those questioned by that party in the Lutheran Church, were considered sufficient indications of the adoption of every tenet of that party. The disapproval of the rite of exorcism at baptism, of private confession before admission to the Lord's table, of the decoration of churches with images, or the approval of the breaking of bread instead of the use of the wafer, the division of the Ten Commandments according to the Heidelberg, not according to the Lutheran, catechism, even the collocation of the two first words of the Lord's prayer, ("unser Vater" for 'Vater unser,") were considered as sufficient indications of the reception of the whole system[1].

by the clergy of the Jena, unless after a formal renunciation of the corruptions there taught, (Id. S. 226.)

[2] Vater, ib. S. 241. It is singular that of these rites, which now became criteria of Lutheranism, some had been before either rejected in the Adiaphoristic controversy, or retained for a time only to avoid offence. (Henke, ib. 470-2.) The very valuable remarks of Whately on the abuse of party-feeling in religion, find ample illustration in those times. It may be here mentioned in confirmation of the ill effect of the indiscriminate use of party names, that the application of that of Calvinist to all, who in the slightest shade varied from the later Lutheran definitions, (Henke, ib. 345.) considerably diminished the numbers of the exclusive party.

The inevitable consequence was, that the parties thus accused of adopting the Reformed doctrines did actually approximate more nearly to them, and the remaining Lutherans became more rigid in their own system and their own peculiarities.

The effect of this narrowing spirit, of these unceasing jarrings, could not but be injurious to the whole Lutheran theology. It is probably the unavoidable consequence of polemics, certainly of such polemics as these, that the question in dispute assumes an undue importance, that the mode of stating the truth, or some collateral points connected with it, more or less displace in the minds of the disputants the practical and religious purport of the doctrines themselves, and their relation to the rest of the Christian system; though in this relation alone, it can exert an efficacious, vital, and consistent influence. Every thing else is forgotten in the determination of the immediate controversy; the conviction of the intellect becomes in itself the end; the heart is forgotten in the exclusive employment of the understanding. What, however, is perhaps only a tendency when other corrections are at hand, was realized in its whole painful extent in the practical as well as the scientific theology of Germany in the 17th century. In proof of this, it will be necessary briefly to consider the different branches of theology as they were, or were not, then studied. A vivid picture of the times can indeed be furnished by no general statement, but must be obtained from the perusal of the authors themselves. Here the results only can be given.

The Reformers, in consistency with their great tenet, that scripture is the only authoritative source of Christian knowledge, had laid the study of the sacred volume as the foundation of all Theological science. In the pursuance of this principle they had established as the rule of interpretation one which, when correctly developed, contains all the elements of right exposition, which have since been gradually vindicated by the combination of several partial efforts. Their, or rather the Biblical, rule, that " Scripture is its own interpreter," includes in itself the religious, historical, grammatical, elements, which were imperfectly, because separately, brought forward by Spener, Semler, and Ernesti. For it is obvious that if scripture is to be understood from itself, those only can rightly and fully understand it who have a mind kindred to that of its author; as any human production, upon which the mind of its author is impressed, will be best understood by him, whose intellectual and moral character is most allied to the original which it expresses. The individual is thus placed, as it were, at the centre of the same circle, from which the views of the author emanated, and contemplates therefore every part in the same order, harmony, and relation, of which they were originally possessed. In religious writings it is plain that the spirit required is a religious spirit; that none can truly understand St. Paul or St. John, whose mind has not been brought into harmony with theirs, has not been elevated and purified by the same spirit with which they were filled: and this, unquestionably, was what the pious Spener meant by his much disputed assertion, that none but the regenerate could understand Holy Scripture. The same principle of the Reformers contained, further, the grammatical element, in that it directed, for the right understanding of the several writers, to the constant comparison with themselves and with each other: views, which were subsequently lost, when it was deemed necessary to inspiration to maintain the perfect purity of the language of the New Testament [1]. Historical, finally, as opposed to the doctrinal, Interpretation, was secured by the direct contrast of this self-illustration of Scripture to the decision of councils, and to the authority of Tradition. If the theory were less distinctly stated, at least it was admirably exemplified in the translation of Luther, and the commentaries of Melanchthon; individual Christian knowledge enabled these Reformers to perceive the fundamental distinctions of the two covenants, to determine what in the documents of the latter was occasioned by temporary events, and, above all, to avoid that iden-

---

[1] It is remarkable, as illustrative of the comparative freedom of judgment in the two Protestant bodies, that the prejudice with regard to the purity of the language of the New Testament, and the importance attached to it, continued predominant among the Lutherans long after it had been extinguished among the Reformed.

tification, by which the full, and pregnant, and varying, language of Scripture is forced into the fetters of the narrowing and monotonous conceptions of system.

These principles of interpretation [1] were for-

---

[1] The much abused doctrine that each passage of Scripture must be interpreted according to the analogia fidei, which was the basis of the dogmatical interpretation, appears as early as in the Clavis Scripturæ Sacræ of the learned but bigoted Flacius. His maxim " omnia debent esse consona catechisticæ, aut articulis fidei" entirely precludes all independent interpretation of Scripture from itself; yet was it received unquestioned in the systematic ultra-Lutheran school. Spener complains of the practice of many of the theologians of his day, who rather made the symbolical books the norm of interpreting Scripture, than Scripture the norm of the symbolical books. (ap. Weism. 1227.) It is therefore natural though remarkable that the Lutheran interpreters of the age immediately subsequent to Luther, who even now retain their value, Strigel, Camerarius, Chemnitz, belonged to the school of Melanchthon; that with the cessation of that school, scriptural interpretation for a time ceased; and that the only three who in the largest portion of the next century were at all distinguished,—J. Gerhard, Tarnov, and Hackspan, were depreciated by their contemporaries, the two latter on the especial account of occasional deviations from received interpretations. (on J. Gerhard, see Weismann (H. E. 2. 1127.) on Tarnov, Budd. Isag. (p. 1669.) on Hackspan and Tarnov, Schröckh (39. 429.) It attests the polemic character of the age that the chief subject of Scriptural exposition was the Apocalypse, (Schr. ib. 428.) and that principally in reference to the Romish Church. Buddeus, speaking generally of the times subsequent to the Reformation, says, Hinc et multum lucis S. S. accessit; licet amplius quid accedere potuisset, nisi simul ortæ in religione dissensiones maximæ gravissimæque multorum animos partium studio infecissent, quo præpediti veritatem illis se offerentem videre aut noluerunt aut non potuerunt. Isag. 1453. § 12.

gotten, this pre-eminence of scriptural above human system strangely reversed by the successors of the Reformers. Scriptural interpretation, instead of being the mistress and guide, became the handmaid, of doctrinal Theology. Its principal and nearly exclusive employment was the justification and defence of the Symbolical books by means of the oft-repeated exposition of the loci classici (beweis-stellen) for each of the positions therein contained, conveyed for the most part in the same technical language; nor was a departure from the received explanations of any of these passages, or a doubt as to the real applicability of one sanctioned as supporting a given doctrine, any more permitted than the rejection of the doctrine itself; or was thought, indeed, to involve it [1]. To this perverted mode of interpretation some ground may have been laid in the Symbolical books themselves, especially in the formula of Concord, in which passages are quoted in proof, whose irrelevancy has been acknowledged by later Lutherans. False ideas of inspiration, introduced by the imaginary necessities [2] of the argument with the Romanists,

---

[1] This fact, which is indeed notorious, is directly asserted by Schröckh. 42, 557. and 43, 6. The influence attributed to the formula of Concord I find also in Meyer Gesch. der Schrifterklärung. B. 2. S. 519. fg.

[2] Bellarmine had inferred from the priority of the existence of the Church to that of Scripture, that the Church could not be founded upon it, but must be the judge and controller of it. The right answer had been that the Church was founded upon Apostolical doctrine, which was faithfully preserved in Scripture alone; that tradition was indeed the foundation of faith, but not

contributed to the same result; from the first assumption, that the whole of Scripture was immediately dictated by the Holy Spirit, was derived a second, that all must be of equal value: to prove this, it was supposed that the same doctrines, the same fundamental truths of Christianity, must be not implied merely, but expressed, by all; a theory which must, of necessity, do much violence to the sacred text, while it overlooked the beautiful arrangement, according to which the different doctrines of Revelation are each prominently conveyed by that mind, which was most adapted to its reception, (love, by St. John; faith, by St. Paul; hope, by St. Peter; faith, developed in works by St. James;) and thus the highest illumination of inspired minds, each in the fullest degree of which it was capable, are combined to convey to us the vast compass of Christian truth. Yet greater confusion must obviously be the result of the same theory, when applied to the Old Testament. The difference of the law and the Gospel, which Luther had so vividly seen, was obliterated, the shadow identified with the substance, the preparatory system with the perfect disclosure. Not content with finding the germs of Christian doctrine in the Old Testament, or those dawning rays, which were to prepare the

as it had become Origenian, Gregorian, &c. but as it was Apostolical, i. e. in Holy Scripture. The answer given was, that as long as the Apostles spoke and taught, their individual agency mingled itself, but that when they began to write, they became the immediate agents and amanuenses of the Holy Spirit.

mental eye for the gradual reception of fuller light, but whose entire character could only be understood by those, who should witness the rising of that luminary whose approach they announced; they not only considered prophecy as being throughout an inverted history, but held that all the distinguishing doctrines of Christianity were even to the Jews as much revealed in the Old Testament as in the New, and that the knowledge of these doctrines was as necessary to their salvation as to ours [1]. No scientific error seems to have prepared so much for the subsequent re-action, in which all prophecy was discarded, all doctrine considered to be precarious.

It was assumed, further, in support of the same system, and was indeed the natural consequence of the doctrinal interpretation, that the same doctrinal word, wherever it occurred, was employed in the same sense; the sense, namely, attached to it in the symbolical books. The Scriptures thus handled, instead of a living Word, could not but become a dead repository of barren technicalities. Less important, lastly, though perhaps in its effects more immediately dangerous, was the corollary to the same theory of inspiration, that even historical passages, in which no religious truth was contained, were equally inspired with the rest, and consequently, that no error, however minute, could even here be admitted. Yet the imparting of religious truth being the object of revelation, any

---

[1] A proof of this will occur in the account of Calixtus, inf.

further extension of inspiration would appear an unnecessary miracle, as indeed it is one no where claimed by the writers of the New Testament. Violence was, in consequence, naturally done to the language of Scripture; it may suffice, as an instance, that ἐκ is by these interpreters stated to be equivalent to εἰς. This, however, for the time, could produce no detrimental doctrinal result, yet in its palpable perversion of the doctrine of Inspiration it did prepare for the indiscriminate rejection of the doctrine itself.

Not only, however, were the principles of scriptural interpretation perverted, but the study itself neglected. At the University of Leipzig, until Spener, one of whose great objects was the promotion of the study of the Bible, obtained a decree from the Elector, directing that an exegetical lecturer should be established, none were there delivered; nor was it without an open expression of bitterness against Spener, that the learned Carpzov, who, on a former occasion, had been compelled, for want of hearers, to abandon his lecture on Isaiah, before he had concluded the first chapter, resumed the attempt [1]. Spener himself mentions, that he knew theologians, who during a six years' course of study at universities, had not heard a single exposition of any biblical book.

The unpractical and untenable character of the doctrinal theology of the same century will have

---

[1] Canstein's Leben Speners, ed. Lange. S. 119. ap Schröckh, 43, 267.

been partly anticipated from what has been already said on the controversies and the scriptural interpretation of the times. It was in fact, for the most part, but a connected polemic; which again, by the method in which it was handled, contributed to reinstate the extremest dryness of scholastic formalism. This method, indeed, was originally reintroduced by contests not so immediately connected with the present view, those with the Romanists, and especially with the Jesuits, who employed the same weapons [1]; but it gained yet greater admission in controversy with individuals, who (as some inclined to the reformed doctrine in the Lutheran Church) endeavoured to conceal diversity of doctrine under similarity of terms. In order to maintain the distinction which it was thought necessary to perpetuate, yet nicer and minuter distinctions were to be adopted, and the contrast of the two systems pursued to its re-

[1] Mosheim, c. 16. s. 3. p. 2. § 19. Budd. Isag. p. 239. and 249, (who, following Elsevich de varia Aristot. in scholis Protestant. fortuna, p. 75, dates the influx of scholasticism from the conference of Ratisbon, 1601.) and Twesten's Dogmatik, S. 235, a work, of which the first volume, which appeared in 1826, is one of the most valuable productions of the new German theology, uniting philosophic depth with pure Christian faith, and which promises, if continued, to form an era in the doctrinal theology of that country. The view of the character of Protestantism, and of its successive stages in Germany, § 8—12, as well as that of doctrinal theology from Melanchthon to the present time, § 13, fgg. though concise, touches in a masterly manner on all the principal points of the enquiry, and has been partly followed by, partly found to coincide with the previous views of, the writer of this essay.

D

motest consequences[1]. It were then almost needless to state, that not even a wish for freedom of enquiry existed; that the Lutheran system, instead of being freed from those errors or unscriptural appendages, which were blended with its basis of scriptural truth, or existed only in the mode of stating what was purely scriptural, was developed, and carried to a precarious height, by increased yet consistent speculation; yet the higher the system was carried, the more dangerous was a return; the fabric was ready to fall by its own weight, yet any attempt to lighten it might only precipitate the evil. The virtual claim of infallibility (which is perhaps natural to every long established, unaltered, Church) was in this case strengthened by the perverted system of Scriptural interpretation. Revelation being interpreted according to the analogy of Faith, or, what was then equivalent, according to the doctrinal system of the Church, could furnish no other result than that which already existed. It was referred to for the justification of preconceived and predetermined opinions. The separation, further, by Calixtus of the system of "Christian moral" from "Christian doctrine," with which it had been hitherto interwoven, though in itself greatly to the advantage of the unity of the latter science, seems to have produced at the time no effect, but that of extinguishing even the sense of the necessity of presenting it in a form influential upon the Christian

---

[1] Twesten, ibid.

life. Abounding then in technical formulæ, (whether from the Aristotelic-scholastic philosophy, or from the scholastic theology) in straw-splitting distinctions, in endless problems and deductions, the systems of the age were rather a massive repertorium of all which might be accumulated on doctrinal theology, than a clear exposition of Christian doctrine itself. No unfavourable specimen of the method is the "systema locorum theologicorum" of the undoubtedly learned Calov[1]. Though he asserts, that he has aimed at conciseness in the questions discussed, the work consists of fourteen quarto volumes; its polemical spirit may be in some measure conceived, in that even the first part, whose professed subject is " the nature of Theology, Religion, divine Revelation, Holy Scripture, and articles of Faith generally," decides that the reformed are to be reckoned among the Heretics, who hold dangerous errors; (Qu. 14, p. 251) and that they are no members of the Augsburg Confession; (Qu. 21, p. 259) and closes with a long censure (p. 881—1216) of the various errors of Calixtus

---

[1] It is no sufficient apology for the defects of this age to insist upon the learning of many of the individuals, who are involved in them. In their mass of knowledge they are equal, often superior, to those of other ages; their deficiency was in the want of scientific spirit, of freedom from prejudice, of comprehensive and discriminating views, without which mere knowledge is useless to the cultivation of science, and oppressive to its possessor. Gerhard's loci Theologici must be excepted from this condemnation, as indeed he himself lived at the commencement of this age.

and his followers. But indeed it is superfluous to state the polemical and bitter character of the work of one, who deemed it necessary to refute, step by step, the commentary of Grotius. The book itself enjoyed all the distinction of its author, until the growing disapprobation of the love of strife, and of a needless creation of heresies, deeply sunk it.

The mode of arranging and of handling the matter thus accumulated, would hardly find place in the present argument, but that it completes the proof of the uninteresting and abstract form with which the whole science was invested. Two favourite methods then of arrangement prevailed, which were for the most part carried through with unvarying uniformity; the causal, and the defining method. The first consisted in enquiring upon each article what were the causæ principales, et minus principales, instrumentales, efficientes, materiales, formales, finales, &c. (that adopted in the above Systema of Calov); the second in premising to each article a definition, which should at the same time comprise the whole doctrine of the Church, and all the opposed heresies: this was then illustrated according to its several parts, was further subdivided, or gave occasion to new definitions, till the whole subject was supposed to be exhausted. Each article was thus split into numerous theses, antitheses, distinctions, questions, objections, &c.[1] Not the ob-

---

[1] Twesten. 236.

scurest nor the most abounding in metaphysical terminology is the " Systema Theologiæ 29 Definitionibus absolutum of J. A. Scherzer; in which the definition concerning Christ occupies three quarto pages in a single period. It thus commences, p. 172, sqq. Christus est θεάνθρωπος, Deus scilicet (etiam αὐτόθεος) et homo, Patri in cœlis et matri Virgini (ut Virgo revera θεοτόκος et Christus etiam secundum humanitatem Filius Dei naturalis sit,) (in terris ὁμοούσιος) constans in unione ad unam personam, (propter quam unionem etiam secundum humanam naturam Filius Dei naturalis, non adoptivus est) [ἀ]περιχωρίϛως, ἀσυγχύτως, ἀτρέπτως, ἀδιαστάτως, ἀχωρίϛως, facta, natura divina et humana impeccabili, &c.[1] Yet these books satisfied all the wants of that age; an acquaintance with the scholastic terminology, and the topics of controversy, with a copious collection of Biblical passages, whose relevance was a point of inferior importance to their numbers was all which the ordinary Theologian required; and the favourite class-book of the age, that most frequently commented upon, and orally expounded, was the dryest and the most meagre, König's[2] Theologia positiva acroamatica synopticè tractata, 1664.

[1] Ap. Schröckh, B. 43, S. 10, 11. There seem to be some misprints, which, not having the original, I cannot correct, but which do not affect the object for which it is quoted.

[2] Buddeus, p. 359, calls it "Skeleton quoddam sine succo et sanguine;" and adds that König heaps unnecessarily metaphysical terms, sometimes incorrectly, and adduces irrelevant scriptural passages, and he attributes its celebrity solely to the then prevalence of

"Christian morals," though separated, as above stated, by Calixtus from doctrinal theology, with which it had been joined rather than combined, (the Christian duties being treated of under the head of the "law" in a species of exposition of the Decalogue; the principle of Christian virtue under the article of Sanctification and the new Obedience[1];) made, as a science, no progress, and was, for the most part, but a relic of the old casuistry[2]. One work alone (Schomer's Specimen Theologiæ Moralis, 1690) contained any traces of scientific method. The rest are very moderate productions. "In the midst of the vehement Theological controversies (says the ecclesiastical historian[3]) which

---

Scholastic Theology. The works which, according to Twesten S. 237, are best calculated to give an image to the Doctrinal Theology of that period, Quenstedt's Theologia didactico-polemica, of the larger, and Baier's Compendium, of the smaller, " are destitute, not indeed of diligence, acuteness, order, and precision, but of unprejudiced scriptural interpretation, philosophical depth, and religious warmth." Quenstedt accounts all, even the most distinguished Theologians, as heretics, who differ in any point, however slight, from those of Wittenberg; Baier can scarcely be understood without a previous thorough knowledge of the then controversies. Budd. ibid.

[1] Twesten, p. 235.
[2] Schröckh, B. 42, p. 558.
[3] Schröckh, B. 43, p. 86. Buddeus states the same fact and the same ground for the degeneracy and defects of books of edification. Fuit ceteroquin jam seculo sexto ea temporum infelicitas ut in certamina et intestinas dissensiones raperentur præstantissima ingenia; unde contingebat ut qui vitæ morumque præcepta inculcabant, minus sapere viderentur. Contemptus ejusmodi librorum, (he adds,) inde auctus est, quod pauci rem

then divided the whole Evangelical Church, was neither time nor room for the scientific treating of theological moral."

A scholastic age has but little feeling for historical enquiry; the neglect, which it experienced in the age of the original schoolmen, again recurred. What did exist was either a mere justification of Protestantism, or historical notices of the contests between the Lutherans and the Reformed; or if more extensive, a catalogue of heretics, which, because opposed to the then orthodoxy, were now also condemned. Yet, for the most part, in the 17th century, the study of ecclesiastical history was, as Spener again complains, at least at the Universities, extinct. The evil consequences of this neglect were subsequently severely felt; history and historical criticism broke upon the age, in which the system began to give way, with a dazzling and perplexing, because unaccustomed, light; they were thought to be, (as indeed every science has been in its first imperfect commencement,) and indeed were in their then state of cultivation, adverse to Revelation. Ignorance of ecclesiastical history had negatively also a detrimental effect; to minds engaged solely in speculation, and accustomed to no system foreign to their own, Christian antiquity wore a strange and unintelligible aspect; unable to divest

serio agere, plurimi contra aut ad gloriolam aut ad lucrum captandum, aut ut mori recepto aliquid darent, talia scribere crederentur. Isag. 588.

themselves of modern ideas, or to transport themselves into times externally so different, the past was to them as a sealed book, and was laid aside without further investigation; the pride of supposed superiority above all preceding times, (the natural consequence of re-awakening energy combined with this ignorance of what antiquity possessed of deeper truth,) was thereby nourished and promoted. Yet was this pride the basis of many of their errors: hence arose the presumptuous contempt with which sentence was passed upon all earlier modes of expression of Christian feeling; hence doctrines, in which the most pious men of old had found the source and nourishment of their piety, were, in the name of eternal reason, determined *à priori* to be prejudicial even to morality; and hence the various and confused dreams of the perfectibility of Christianity. A large portion, also, of Christian evidence was lost, from the consequent failure to understand the manner, in which the influence of Christianity exerted itself. Equally a consequence of the same neglect was the positive error of, unconsciously at least, theorizing on events, ideas, persons, of antiquity, as if in all respects similar to those of modern times; with a little modification, the well-known severe terms of Göthe would apply to many besides the wretched Bahrdt, Da kam mir ein Gedanke von ungefähr, So redete ich, wenn ich Christus wäre [1].

The Theological sciences, whose application

---

[1] In his Bahrdt.

forms the basis of practical Theology, being thus perverted or obliterated; the exposition of Scripture, and Christian doctrine converted into polemics; ecclesiastical history, so pre-eminently the magistra vitæ, and Christian Moral, forgotten; it could scarcely be but that this crown, as it has been justly called, of all theology [1] should equally suffer. From the nature, however, of Pastoral Theology, those two portions alone which partake of a scientific character, the pulpit and catechetical instruction, can furnish results sufficiently definite or universal, from which to attempt, without risk of injustice, to form an estimate of the general condition of the whole church. Each of these was injured by the predominant importance attached to controverted points. Elementary instruction, as far as other interests permitted it still to be cultivated, was perverted from its proper object, the communication of the essentials of Christianity, to the enforcement of the system of the Church in the immense compass of its abstract articles. Illustration and defence of contested points displaced the inculcation of vital truths in their practical import; the inexperienced mind was oppressed and bewildered by the exposition of points which belonged only to systematic Theology [2]; the er-

[1] Schleiermacher Darstell. des Theol. Studiums, § 8.
[2] See Schröckh (43, 154.) who mentions that in the illustration of many Catechisms of this age, one, or even several octavo volumes, filled with a complete doctrinal system, were employed.

ror, at all times natural to the human mind, of regarding religion as a matter of memory, was rendered almost inevitable by the indiscriminate mode in which the whole sum of doctrine was propounded. Yet more common, however, was the opposed extreme, by which catechizing, was either, as in the original scholastic age [1], neglected, or was committed to subordinate persons, as a mere mechanical labour. In Saxony, which more indeed than the rest of Germany was the seat of a dead orthodoxism, it was not without much ridicule that Spener, when appointed Court-Preacher and member of the Consistory at Dresden, revived it [2]; not without the taunt that "the elector had sent for a Court-Preacher, and had received a school-master." Yet to this failure of catechising, whatever success unbelief had among the lower and middling classes (positive unbelief was, however, among them rare) is far more attributable, than to any direct attempts of a later unbelieving clergy or of profligate Rationalist writers [3]. The house was swept and gar-

---

[1] Catecheticæ Theologiæ, says Buddeus (Isag. p. 332,) eo tempore quo scholasticum illud regnum floruit, nulla fere habita fuit ratio; ideoque hinc inde quædam solum ejus vestigia deprehendere licet. Id quod, (he truly adds, and it is a warning criterion for every age,) corruptæ admodum ac depravatæ hisce seculis ecclesiæ documentum præbet luculentum.

[2] Schröckh, ibid.

[3] This subject will occur more fully hereafter; here it may suffice to notice that Bahrdt, the only one of the infidel writers who had any influence on the middling classes, was no Theologian. His frivolity and charlatanism, combined with powers of

nished; it was abandoned, empty, and undefended; it remained but for the master to enter in. The coldness of unbelief is preferable to the lukewarmness of such a state, in that it is more easily recoverable.

Not neglected, indeed, but for the most part destitute of practical spirit, was the other ordinary medium of Christian instruction, the pulpit. The different proportions which the several parts of divine service bear in Germany, (where the prayers, including the hymns, occupy a much smaller space, and much less of Scripture is read than among ourselves), have from the beginning given a primary importance to this ministerial intercourse of the pastor with his flock; and this the more, as the occasions of these addresses are more frequent, in that they are delivered at all the occasional services,—baptism, marriage, burial of the dead, and the public confessional on the day preparatory to the participation in the communion, as well as at confirmation, and in the ordinary service of the Lord's day. Luther, accordingly, who knew and assigned it its importance, purified it from all its previous defects, and provided in his Kirchenpostille, which he deemed his best work[1], a model for future preachers. The interest of polemics seems, however, soon to have

imagination and an easy style, gave him, for a time, access and popularity among the superficial, who were willing to be deceived. He had, however, no share in the Theological revolutions of the period.

[1] Schröckh, 39. 460.

swallowed up every other; nor, with the exception of Mathesius, does the name of any distinguished preacher occur among the successors of Luther. Of those who wrote on the theory of Christian oratory, a disciple of Melanchthon's alone, Hemming [1], extended his views beyond the mere external arrangement. The history of every controversy after the Reformation gives the proof that intemperate disputation on abstract questions had largely displaced Christian instruction. Early in the seventeenth century this became systematic; the preacher not unnaturally taught that, in which alone he had been himself instructed, and which he had been inured to think of primary or exclusive importance; he delivered it in the same scholastic terminology in which he had himself received it [2]. Not orthodoxy, then, was wanting in the sermons of the seventeenth century, but the developement of that orthodoxy in its influence on Christian practice. Moral, when preached, being separated from implied, equally as from express, reference to the Christian truths, was dry and barren; and the acknowledgment of these truths manifested itself solely in the refutation of heretics. The sermons printed by James Andrea, minister at Erlangen, 1568, may furnish a specimen of the usual subjects of these discourses. They consist of four divisions; 1. Of the division between Lutherans and Papists;

---

[1] In his Pastor, 1566. See Schröckh, 464.
[2] Other defects are mentioned by Schröckh, ib.

2. Of the Church of Christ and the Zwinglians; 3. Against the Schwenkfeldians; 4. Against the Anabaptists. To shew the spirit of these polemics, may suffice the following commencement of those of Artomedes of Königsberg (1590) on the Lord's Supper. " Against the holy Communion war two raging armies of the incarnate devil; on the one side the ungodly Papists, on the other the over-curious and conceited Calvinists. The wretched heathen Ovid is a better theologian than our Calvinists." There follow yet stronger and more offensive expressions. The style was equally repulsive. The ordinary divisions were a dry grammatical exposition of Scriptural texts, and a polemical or so-called practical application, equally uninteresting and uninfluential. It is of course impossible to multiply instances; suffice one of Hermann of Brieg in Silesia, on the Gospel of the day, the history of Zacchæus. The text selected was, " He was little of person." The division of the sermon was, 1. The word " He" teaches us, "personæ qualitatem;" 2. " was," " vitæ fragilitatem;" 3. " little," " staturæ parvitatem." The practical application was, 1. Zacchæus est informator de varietate operum Dei; 2. consolator parvorum; 3. adhortator ut defectum nostrum virtute compensemus. There were indeed some splendid exceptions of men, as Arndt[1], J. V. Andreá, and J. Gerhard, who kept aloof from

---

[1] Arndt's " True Christianity" was the substance of his sermons. His lectures on Luther's Catechism are also a memorial of his practical piety.

polemics, and whose piety has been venerated by every subsequent age, and has edified many other churches[1]. "But these instances," adds the historian, "besides that they were exceptions from the usual course, influenced the whole but little; and Homiletic [2] remained a science almost entirely unknown to those who deemed that they most excelled in it[3]."

More, however, of the scientific and practical defects, or rather offences, of the theological preparation of that age, may be learnt from the testimonies of two men of very different characters, Spener and Thomasius; the former a divine, mildly mourning in heartfelt pain over the decay of piety, and of the practical study of theology; the latter, the celebrated reformer of the evangelical ecclesiastical law, with some, though not undeserved, mockery. Spener, in his Pia Desideria, and the preface to Dennhauer's Hodosophia, gives the following account of the preparatory and professional studies of theologians. "In the seminaries for the most part, Latin alone is taught; Greek extremely seldom; Hebrew not at all: persons come to the Universities without having an idea of the nature of Theology, which is consi-

---

[1] Gerhard's Meditations is, with Arndt's Christianity, among the few books which have been valued by every age and country. Buddeus (ib. 588.) mentions translations into German, French, English, Polish, and Swedish.

[2] Christian rhetoric, the art of preaching, of Christian persuasion and instruction.

[3] Schröckh, ib. 468.

dered a mere matter of memory; hence all prayer, all meditation, all attention to a holy life, is wanting. Philosophy is a dry scholastical assemblage of formulas; to it is most time devoted. Philology is almost unknown. Many theologians do not understand the New Testament in Greek. The most important Theological science is thetik (doctrinal Theology in its confined sense); scriptural grounds for the doctrines are not deemed necessary. Scriptural interpretation is learnt after entering on the office of preacher, in order to write the expository part of the sermon, which contains a mere dialectical explanation. Next to thetik is polemic[1] the most important science, though it is melancholy to contend against error when one knows not the truth. And if polemic must be carried on, yet should it be as in the state, where one class only is engaged in war. Ethics are not taught at all; homiletic consists only in a philosophical schematism, how a sermon is logically to be arranged." The remarks of Thomasius are conveyed in the following description of a candidatus theologiæ[2]. "He has for two years

---

[1] " Joined with doctrinal Theology," (says Schröckh, describing this age, 39. 482, sq.) " was polemic theology considered the highest dignity of the theologian; and, under a biblical expression, ' to carry on the wars of the Lord,' was the field in which he most readily appeared, fully armed for the defence of the province entrusted to him. That such a constant readiness and inclination to fight, often, as in the political world, brought on wars which might easily have been avoided, cannot be denied."

[2] "In his Freymüthige lustige und ernsthafte, jedoch Vernunft-

studied the Aristotelic philosophy; in the third, positive theology; in three more, that of the schoolmen; and in the four last, which he has spent at the University, polemic: he has held a long disputation on the use of metaphysics in the refutation of heretics; is able, by means of those different species of theology, the concordance, and the skeletons, to give, at an hour's preparation, a well constituted sermon; is employed, besides, on a refutation of that infernal book, Ric. Simonis Critical History of the Old Testament; but in practical or moral theology is an entire stranger." No wonder then that Spener should meet at least with assent in his earnest regrets, which he expressed, however, with his peculiar mildness[1]: " That the clergy needed an entire reformation, and so much the more, in that their defects were not acknowledged; that many of them were wholly strangers to earnest inward piety, conceiving that every thing was comprised in skill in religious disputation; that much foreign useless matter, many needless niceties, had been introduced into theology; whence many theologians, when they attained an office, could make no use of what they had learnt; that it was necessary to study holy Scripture with much more diligence than had

---

und Gesetzmässige Gedanken über allerhand, fürnemlich aber neue, Bücher." ap. Schröckh, 42, 561.

[1] See the observations of Weism. ib. 1168, sq. where, in praising Spener's great wisdom and moderation, he mentions that many thought rather that he did too little than too much.

been hitherto done, to put a due limit to religious controversies, and to educate and form future ministers upon an entirely different plan, reminding them, that much more depended upon a pious life than upon their diligence and study; lastly, that sermons should be made more useful[1]." No wonder that H. Müller should speak against the four dumb church-idols, the font, the pulpit, the confessional, and the communion-table[2]; or that the result should be that described by the truly pious, able, and learned Joh. Gerhard, "that the most diligent church-goers were guilty of the most reckless practices; but if one did not admit them to be good Christians, they threatened an action for libel, and whoever recommended earnest Christianity, was termed Pharisee, Weigelian, and Rosecrucian[3]."

Such a system could not endure; it contained within itself the seeds of its own dissolution; a

---

[1] Pia desideria ap. Schröckh, ib. p. 549.

[2] The censures passed upon him by Joh. Müller of Hamburg for these expressions seemed, even to those times, captious and unjust. Fateor (says Weismann, ib. p. 1143) multum hujus viri existimationi apud me detrahere acta ejus eristica, et planè superflua, cum optimo Viro, H. Mullero, cui plures alii et celebres nostræ Ecclesiæ Theologi assistebant contra censuram Hamburgensem. Cp. Buddeus, who mentions some of his defenders, and says, that his writings omnium fere promeruerunt calculum (ib. 590.) H. Müller's Erquickungsstunden, especially, long continued to be one of the principal practical works of Germany.

[3] The evidences on this head will hereafter be occasionally increased by the incidental mention of some of the innovations in doctrines which the ultra-Lutheran party opposed.

re-action was almost the unavoidable consequence, unless some one, or some succession of men, gifted with Luther's pious and discriminating mind, should establish a separation between this accumulation of narrowing human definitions and the simple truths of the Gospel, should replace by the influential faith of the heart the barren contentious scholasticism, by which the understanding alone was occupied, or rather was distracted. It was the natural effect of a system, in itself partly untenable, and of which every untenable point was developed to its utmost extent by other deductions and hypotheses, to provoke the inconsiderate rejection of a whole, whose every part was maintained with equal decision, and as of equal importance; it was the direct tendency of the endless disputes about abstract points, in which the different parties were agreed about nothing, but that unquestioned certainty might be arrived at, and that they were each in possession of that certainty, that distaste and doubt of the whole should be engendered; it was the natural consequence of so vast a system of abstract doctrine, apparently influential in the production of discord alone, that the authority of the whole should be questioned: to what purpose, it would be asked, should so vast a body of doctrine be made known to mankind, some of which in its own nature can have no influence, and the rest has none? doubt of the whole would further be excited by the manifestly weak or distorted basis, upon which much was rested;

aversion would be created by some unscriptural doctrines, repugnant to the nature of God[1]; opposition by the intolerance of their supporters[2]: there are few probably who would not have been confirmed in their difficulties by such an antagonist as Göze, who seems to have sought a triumph over, rather than the conviction of his sceptical, but probably more Christian[3] opponent.

[1] It may suffice to mention that of the eternal condemnation of the heathen, which appears to have been generally held by the orthodox. This appears more strikingly from the fact that Schröckh uniformly mentions as a peculiarity in the system of any doctrinal writer, even a doubt of its truth, than from any number of instances with which I may myself have met. To give one instance, Schröckh names as a freedom of opinion in Spener, unexpected in his times, and which, therefore, was interpreted to his injury, that " he doubted not that even out of the Evangelical Church, not children only, but many of maturer age, would be saved." (Theol. Bedenken ap. Schr. 43, 281.) The maintenance of the contrary opinion gave rise to one infidel work at least, Eberhard's Neue Apologie des Socrates; even Ernesti expresses a doubt whether the happiness of virtuous heathens and Jews be consistent with the importance of the Christian Revelation. Neue Theol. Biblioth. 1. B. S. 105. 5. B. S. 359.

[2] This is mentioned by Schlegel also (Kirchengesch, 5. B. S. 247.) as one of the causes of the unbelief of the 18th century in Germany.

[3] I know not any man whose scepticism gives one more pain, excites more regret, than that of Lessing. His works manifest a conscientious desire after truth, a struggle to extricate himself from his difficulties; he first pointed out the impregnable bulwark of religion against all scientific objections, which has since been philosophically justified, that the foundation, the *original* seat of religion is in the feeling, not in the understanding. Without subscribing to every thing contained in the following passages, it

Other causes actually coincided, but these furnished a well prepared soil for the seed of unbe-

may be permitted to cite them, to shew what the heart of the individual was, whom the unhappy circumstances of his time, and the intolerance of his opponents seem mainly to have driven into scepticism. They are collected in the often-quoted work, Twesten's Dogmatik, p. 19. Under the word " Religion," (in his posthumous works) he says, " The many works which in modern times appear in defence of the Christian religion, are open to the objection, not only that they prove very ill what they undertake to prove, but that they are quite contrary to the spirit of Christianity, in that its truth is such as rather to be felt, than to be made an object of intellectual knowledge." (Collectan. Werke, Th. 16. S. 305.) Hence, (observes T.,) he makes a clear distinction between the Theologian and the Christian; the former, he supposes, may be perplexed by certain objections, which threaten to shake the props by which he would support religion, " but what do this man's hypotheses, and explanations, and proofs, concern the Christian?" He possesses already the Christianity which he *feels* to be so true, and in which he himself is so blessed. When the paralytic *experiences* the beneficial shocks of the electric spark, what matters it to him whether Nollet, or Franklin, or neither, be in the right? (Zusätze zu der Wolf. Fragm. Werke, Th. 5. S. 18.) To the same purport against Göze. (Th. 6. S. 16.) " Even supposing one should not be able to remove all the objections, which reason is so busy in making against the Bible, yet religion would still remain undisturbed and unconcerned in the hearts of those Christians, who had attained an inward *feeling* of its essential truths." Again, Axiomat. (Th. 6. S. 77.) " He, whose heart is more Christian than his head, pays not the slightest regard to those objections, since he *feels* what others content themselves with thinking." (cp. S. 139, at greater length.) " This appeal (adds T.) to the *feeling* of the facts of inward Christianity is Lessing's leading idea in the contest with Göze ; and how much he was in earnest, might be shewn from many passages of his writings, and the whole frame of his mind."

lief, under whatever immediate circumstances it might be planted.

The first opposition to this system, however, came from other quarters. It seems as if it were not until other methods had been employed in vain, that the storm of unbelief was allowed to burst over so much of this fair portion of the Christian Church; not until they had refused to return from the light of their self-kindled fire, to the sun of pure Christianity; that that sun was for a time obscured to them, in order that the temporary privation might make them more deeply feel its value, and benefit by its light and warmth and healing.

In the very beginning of the 17th century, the destructive effects [1] of the existing system in substituting dialectic disquisition for practical Christianity, had been felt by two theologians, Prætorius, minister of Salzwedel, (ob. 1610), and the ever-memorable and pious Arndt. (ob. 1611). The latter alone had a very wide permanent influence [2], of

---

ib. p. 20. The late Rennell (Notes on the Conversion of Count Struensee, p. 20,) and Coleridge. (Aids to Reflection, p. 136,) have given seasonable advice to those, who think that in the reception of Christianity the intellect alone is concerned.

[1] Arndt's " true Christianity" was occasioned by the prevailing corruptions; its object was to shew that " true Christianity consists in the manifestation of a true, living, active, faith, in genuine piety, and the fruits of righteousness." Buddeus in the passage following that quoted Sup. p. 38. n. 3. assigns the exclusive polemic as the source of these corrupt manners.

[2] Spener, however, in his candid judgment of Prætorius, mentions the " very many instances of pious and orthodox men,

which, however, as is generally the case of the most extensive usefulness, the largest results were late, and long after his own personal removal[1]. In his life-time, though he united all the humility and mildness of Spener with the firmness in which the latter was deficient, though he entered not into the polemics of his time, and his exertions were calculated to replace, not to overthrow, the existing system, he was the object of dislike and persecution. Even while these exertions were limited to the exercise of his ministry, he was accused of the heresy of requiring from Christians Angelic perfection, and of practising alchemy; his extensive benevolence was attributed to the discovery of the philosopher's stone. The clergy of Brunswick issues warnings against the " poison" of Arndt[2]. The immortal work on " True Christianity," (1605), which was translated into every language of Europe, and has been valued by pious minds of every succeeding age, did but increase the hostility. A host of antagonists charged him with heresy, termed his writings jugglery, himself an unlearned presuming fool[3]. L. Osiander

who, next to Scripture, ascribe almost all their Christian knowledge to him." ap. Weism., 1193.

[1] Weism., 1178. S. 8.
[2] Weism., ib. 1175.
[3] The names of some of his opponents may be found in Weism. 1176, and Budd., ib. 614. Though a few were distinguished in the controversies of their time, they have long been forgotten. They were mostly inferior, even in learning, to the great man whom they reviled. See Schröckh 39,450, and Weism. 1174, who

pronounced, that they could not be read by the ignorant without risk of salvation; that they were full of heretical poison, pestilential, abounding in Papism, Calvinism, Flacianism, Schwenkfeldianism, and Weigelianism [1]. He accused him of blasphemy against the Holy Spirit, and of ascribing the agency of God to the devil; by others were added Osiandrism, Paracelsism, and the use of the language of the mystico-chemical philosophers [2]; it was made a crime that he did not bind himself, in his religious teaching, to the symbolical formulæ; he was charged with using expressions in common with earlier mystics or fanatics, who had spoken against a bare outward Church formalism [3]. These imputations in part refuted themselves, in part did not need refutation; he was cleared of all error of moment by subsequent divines of his own Church [4]; and his own valuable

speaks of his " eruditio planè singularis et arcana etiam in partibus doctrinæ Theologiam non concernentibus." The source of the accusation was, that he did not employ it in the same ostentatious and unedifying manner which was usual in the sermons of the time. (See Schröckh, ib. 464.)

[1] In his " Theologisches Bedenken und Christlich treu-herzig Erinnerung, welcher Gestalt Arndt's wahres Christenthum nach Anleitung des Heiligen Worts zu betrachten sey." 1623. Weismann, however, mentions, that he is said to have retracted at the approach of death. (ib. 1176.)

[2] Mosheim, c. 17. 11. 2. 1. 39. Weismann, l. c.

[3] Vater, p. 258—9. Weism. (p. 1177), as well as others ap. Budd. 613, doubts not that he conferred a benefit on the Church by extracting and combining with Scripture what was really solid and useful in the mystic or practical authors.

[4] Besides others who vindicated him, among whom was the

work has, in better times, produced far more than a mere negative testimony. His principal immediate influence, however, seems to have been among the laity [1]: upon the system of the German Church he acted most extensively through the formation of the mind of Spener, whose character was principally framed by the early study of Arndt's "True Christianity [2]," in combination with two English works.

The thirty last years, however, of the half-century, which intervened between the death of Arndt and the commencement of Spener's public exertions, witnessed an attack upon the system on the scientific side, which, however its immediate operation was annihilated by the heat of the parties, prepared for its subsequent downfal by leading to historical enquiry, to a better scriptural interpretation, and to a more practical view of controversy.

valuable J. Gerhard, who regarded him as a second parent, (Weism. 1177) the praise of the otherwise bigoted Hulsemann, the bitter opponent of Calixtus, of Dannhauer, (at first prejudiced against Luther as well as against Arndt,) and of M. Geier, who attributes to his work his own real Christianity, will be above suspicion of undue attachment. (Weism., ib. cp. Budd. 614.)

[1] Two highly-gifted authors, however, were formed by him; Scriver (Superintendant at Magdeburg, died at Quedlinburg, 1693, as first court-preacher,) whose Seelenschatz, or Considerations on Doctrine and Morals, was one of the most valued edifying books of the time: (Schröckh, B. 42. p. 87.) and H. Müller of Rostock, already mentioned.

[2] Spener mentions that Arndt was the only modern besides Luther, whom he quoted by name in his preaching. (ap. Weism. 1192.)

Nearly coincident with the conclusion of the unequalled horrors of the thirty years' war, (a war whose length and miseries might long before have been closed but for the disunion of the two Protestant parties, and the jealousy of a Lutheran court-preacher and adviser of Joh. George I. of Saxony[1]), was the signal for the Syncretis-

[1] The principles expressed on this occasion, alone, entitle it to notice. M. Hoe von Hoënegg, the individual in question, persuaded his patron, that " an union with the Papists was better and safer than one with the reformed," (Leyser Bedenken daruber von Hoe herausgeg, 1619. &c. ap. Henke, iii. 487.) and that Bohemia " should not be exposed to be devoured by the Calvinistic Antichrist;" (Hoe's letter in Unschuld. Nachr. (1714.) S. 39. ap. Henke, ibid.) which confirms the statement of the experienced Cardinal Bentivoglio, (many years employed by Rome in Flanders and France,) that the Lutherans were more disinclined to the Reformed than to the Romanists. (Lettres de Bentivoglio, p. 42.) Hoe, though moderated by the necessities of the times during the conference of Leipzig, (1631), resumed his former tone when hopes of a separate Lutheran peace reappeared, wrote against a hundred points, in which the Reformed held erroneous, nay, Arian opinions, (Unvermeidl. Rettung wider das Oraculum Dodonæum, &c. 1635), and dissuaded from every effort to procure their religious freedom. (Henk. ib. 491.) The Reformed, as their theology remained free from formularism to a much later period than that of the Lutherans, and unbelief found consequently a much slower access among them, so were they throughout more tolerant. Public reconciliation was never hindered by them ; private polemics were but seldom bitter. Besides the resolution of the famous Synod of Charenton (1631), the conference of Cassel (1661) was approved of by the most distinguished theologians even of the Dutch Church ; (see authorities ap. Henk. iv. 276.) and at the very time that Hoe was making the above exertions, Pareus wrote to promote the concord of the two churches, met, however, with refu-

tic [1] controversy given by Buscher in his work tations only from the Lutherans. (Henk. 3. 485; Schröckh, 40. 194.) The name of Evangelical was denied them, (Wittenb. Bedenken, ap. Henk. 4. 279.) The conference of Cassel was condemned by most Lutherans, by some as a conspiracy to betray the truth to apostasy and ungodliness, (Henke, ib. 277-9.) though it asserted only, that the difference of the two churches did not affect the foundation of faith nor salvation. (ib. 275.) In the same spirit they had rejected the proposals for peace from the Synod of Lissa (1645) as treacherous; (Consil. theol. Witteb. i. 527) and in conformity to the response of the University of Wittenberg, refused, at the ensuing conference with the Romanists at Thorn, to unite in worship with the Reformed. (Henke, ib. 257, 8.) In Brandenburg, the so called Nominal-Elenchus, or the preaching by name against the characteristic doctrines of the Reformed, was held part of the duty of the clergy; (ib. 279.) and many of them abandoned their functions and their land sooner than comply with the moderate requisition of the wise and excellent Elector, Frederic William the Great, that both parties should abstain from invidious deductions from the Confessions of the other, &c.; and that the Exorcism at Baptism should be omitted, when requested by both parents. (see ap. Henk. 280, 1.) Among these zealots one regrets to see Paul Gerhard, the author of the most beautiful and pious hymns in the German Church. To close these painful instances, in Swedish Pomerania, where were no Reformed, an order from the local authorities, suspending declamations against them, and erasing from the Liturgy the petition, " Repress the Turks, Papists, and Calvinists," was annulled by application to Stockholm; and the intermarriage of a Lutheran with a Reformed declared inadmissible, (more such cases in Balthasar von d. Eifer d. Pommern gegen d. Reformirten ap. Henk. ib. 283.) Some knowledge of the relation of the two churches is necessary both to understand the vehemence of the opposition to Calixtus, and as one specimen of the state of polemics in the Lutheran Church.

[1] An invidious meaning was given to the term Syncretism by means of a false etymology, as if its promoters wished for a mix-

against Calixtus; " Crypto-Papismus novæ theologiæ Helmstadiensis." (1639.) Seldom has any one been so much misunderstood, partly perhaps from his own unguardedness [1], but principally from the passions of his opponents, as this great and penetrating man. Incidental expressions in works, of which the substance alone [2] was his, were caught up and imputed as heresies; real positions [3] perverted, and made to bear upon some existing or extinct heresy; his anxiety to promote Christian charity converted into indifferentism. Though his office

---

ture of religions. It implied the reverse; for it was used, in its original sense, of union in a great common object *notwithstanding* existing differences, having been first employed by Greek authors, of similar conduct in the " *Cretans.*"

[1] See Weism. p. 1195. §. 3. Possessed of great talent, and taking comprehensive views, he was not aware until too late that every expression would be thus sifted.

[2] This was the case with most of his works: among them the Epitome Theologiæ was published, from his lectures, unrevised, and without his knowledge. In this occurred once, and once only, the expression, that " God could only be called indirectly, improperly, and per accidens the cause of sin;" alluding to the passages in which God is said to harden men's hearts. An impious sense was given to the phrase, whereas it implies, that God cannot, in any proper sense, be called the author of sin. (See Weism. ib. p. 1260.)

[3] Much occasion of offence was, for instance, taken at his allowing to the fathers of the five first centuries a *secondary* authority in fundamental articles of faith. This, which in fact in no respect differed from the practice of all Protestant writers, who have uniformly referred to the agreement of the early fathers, as witnesses of the primitive faith, was imputed to him as involving the Romanist error of setting human authority co-ordinate with Scripture. (See Weism. ibid. p. 1195, 6.)

as teacher of theology was conferred upon him for his success in controversy with a Romanist[1], and though by one of themselves[2] he is named as their ablest antagonist, his Lutheran brethren charged him with secretly favouring them; though he wrote against the distinguishing doctrines of the Reformed, and even represented them to be self-contradictory[3], he was accounted to belong to them; Arianism and Judaism[4] were imputed

---

[1] The Jesuit Aug. Turrianus had nearly effected the conversion of a young nobleman of Brunswick, but withdrew after one day's conference with Calixtus. Calixtus was then twenty-seven. Schröckh, 39. 690, 1.

[2] Bossuet Traité de la Communion sous les 2 espêces, p. 1. §. 62. p. 12. Calixtus' works immediately upon this subject were, those on the Sacrifice of the Mass, on the Infallibility of the Pope, on the Marriage of the Clergy, (a treatise of considerable historical research, and the first upon the subject), and especially the Digressio, qua excutitur nova ars Bart. Nihusii, written upon the sophistical position then popular among French theologians, that the Catholics, by right of prescription, had no occasion to prove their doctrines, but that the Protestants, as plaintiffs, must disprove them, and that from the simple words of Scripture without inferences. This, however, was by no means the sole subject of the work, it gave occasion to lay down general principles proving the unjustified introduction of several of the distinguishing Romanist doctrines, &c.

[3] Disput. xi. de Cœna Domini, p. 247, sq. and more generally in the Annott. et Animadvr. in Confessionem Reform. Thorunii in Colloquio A. 1645 oblatam, &c. 1655.

[4] These charges were brought by Weller, "Teutsche Probe." Scharff of Wittenberg imputed to him enormous errors against the Trinity, and almost Photinianism; and so others. (Weism. ib. 1096, 7.) In the same spirit Reinboth was accused of an approximation to Socinianism and Atheism, for holding that the

to him, because he thought that the doctrine of the Trinity was not revealed with equal clearness in the Old as in the New Testament; nor was, under the old dispensation, necessary to salvation. Such, however, and others, though the subjects, were not the ground of attack; they were the channels in which it flowed, the stream which filled them was his supposed indifference to the distinguishing doctrines of Lutheranism. It would now scarcely appear credible that this charge of indifferentism arose, not in any of the attempts, which have been renewed from time to time in every country, to unite different confessions; (this Calixtus thought then impossible, or at least distinctly stated, that he did not aim[1];) but in the endeavour to revive a mutual Christian feeling, by recalling to mind, that, however important the points of disagreement, still both Lutheran and Reformed, nay, the Romanist, held all the doctrines necessary to salvation. Beyond this Calixtus did not go; he shewed by his writings and by his actions his value for the Lutheran doctrine; but he did wish, that amid this diversity the ground of unity should not be forgotten; that, amid the names of Lutheran, Reformed, and Romanist, that of Christian should not be obliterated; nor in his very widest assertion, that all doctrines necessary

---

doctrine of the Procession of the Holy Spirit from the Son was not a necessary article, nor prescribed in the ancient Creeds. Henk. iv. 264.

[1] See Schröckh, 704, sq. Weism. ib. 1203. sq.

to salvation are contained in the Apostles' Creed, (however in shallower minds such a maxim may at different times have been a cloak for indifferentism) was there any undervaluing of the main Christian doctrines; since it was evidently not a mere abstract belief in the Father, Son, and Holy Spirit, but that of the doctrines therein involved, which he understood. This meaning he has himself sufficiently explained [1]. The conference at Thorn, between the two Protestant bodies and the Romanist Church, where his presence as coadjutor of the Reformed delegates, at the request of the Elector of Brandenburg, gave ground to lasting offence, had in view only the same general object, that a better acquaintance with each other's principles might diminish the bitterness of discord [2]. Half the evils of controversy would indeed cease, did the mass of each party derive their knowledge of the tenets of their opponents from any other source than the refutations on their own side. Calixtus promised the same assistance to some of the Lutheran delegates, but

---

[1] Calixtus' meaning is clear from other passages, where he expresses the same sentiment in different language, as, that all a Christian need believe in order to salvation was contained in the ancient creeds and decisions of the councils; that whoever agreed with these doctrines of the ancient Church, he was in heart united with him, &c. (Digress. de arte novâ, p. 462, sq. ap. Schröckh, 39. 697.) See especially the principles developed in the De Tolerantia Reformator.

[2] The points of controversy were in this conference neither to be attacked nor defended, but to be explained; the word " dis-

was, by means of others, rejected[1]. In this Christian career he was acting on the principles and according to the oath of the professors of his University to promote Christian peace[2], and, from his personal knowledge of the character of the different confessions in various countries[3], his mind became alive to the existence of the same great doctrines in all, to which his contemporaries had been deadened by exclusive attention to points of controversy. The endless struggles in

pute" was not to be used; it was to be a fraterna collatio, a colloquium charitativum. It had also the result, that the Reformed Church, especially that of Brandenburg, did here form the Confession, called, from the conference, that of Thorn. (Schröckh, 39. 509—12. Henk. iv. 256-9.) After this conference many of the orthodox party ceased to regard Calixtus as an evangelical teacher. (Schröckh 39. 702. fg.)

[1] Schröckh, 39. 703.

[2] Mosh. c. 17. ii. 2. § 21. Weismann says that Helmstadt had always exerted a greater freedom of opinion than other Universities, which accordingly denied to its theologians the character of pure and genuine Lutherans, contrary to their own protestations. The non-reception of the Formula of Concord seems in part to have contributed to this difference; the doctrine of the ubiquity of Christ's body, whose rejection appeared to the Lutherans of that formula to involve an approximation to the Reformed doctrine, was not only not admitted, but expressly set aside by Luther in one of his later works, (quoted by Calixtus de Tolerantia Reformator. ap. Schrockh. 39. 497.)

[3] He studied the practical character of the reformed confession in Holland, in England, (where he derived much benefit from Casaubon, and his attention was directed to the study of the fathers by the English bishops), and in France. At Cölln, where practical Romanism was most fully exhibited, he employed six months. (See his life in Schröckh, 39. 689-91.)

which Calixtus became involved, prevented his giving a better direction to theological study by the complete digestion of his own comprehensive views, and limited his immediate influence nearly to the countries where the Formula of Concord had not been introduced [1]; yet many of his opinions produced enquiry [2]; historical investiga-

[1] Such as Holstein, Brunswick, and part of Hesse Nurnberg. The whole University of Helmstadt coincided with Calixtus; among whose members Conring, the most distinguished and most variously cultivated of the learned of his country, (Schröckh, ib. 707) through his influence with different princes, by whom he was constantly consulted, was enabled to remove many of the imputations circulated against him. The duchess Anna Sophia procured admission for theologians of his school into Brandenburg. (see authorities ap. Henke, iv. 271-3.) In Saxony, on the contrary, among other places, no one who had studied at Helmstadt was preferred, without abjuring the so-called Calixtian principles. (Answer of Fred. Will. of Brand. ap. Henk. ib. 280.) Among other attempts of a similar character, most worthy of notice is that of Calov, who endeavoured, by means of a new symbolical book, to exclude the Calixtians from the Lutheran Church and the religious peace. (See Weism. ib. 1205-6. Henke, iv. 268.) Even in Königsberg, where they were protected by the Elector of Brandenburg, all the influence of his disciples was destroyed by the vehement opposition of Mislenta, popular tumult excited, and even an honourable burial refused to M. Behm, who would not unite in decrying them. (Hartknoch Preuss. Kirchenh. S. 609. ff. and others ap. Weism. ib. 1205. Henk. iv. 268-9.)

[2] His view, for instance, on the Revelation of the doctrine of the Trinity in the Old Testament, and on the supposed necessity of its being believed under the former dispensation, led naturally to inquiry into the now almost obliterated distinction of the two covenants, and into the gradual character of revelation; the limitation which he introduced into the doctrine of inspiration, confining it

tion[1] and a sounder scriptural interpretation commenced, through his example, instruction, or principles; his fragment on the study of theology contained and illustrated his valuable and large views on the nature of the necessary preliminary[2] acquirements, as well as on the compass and order of the different branches of the science itself; and in the separation of essentials from non-essentials, his warnings against needless controversy, and his opposition to a dead faith[3], he directly pre-

to the essentials of religion, and admitting the existence of minor errors of transcription, must tend to a simplification of the existing theory; his exclusion of the doctrines of universal religion from the sum of Christian truths, would naturally lead to more defined ideas on Revelation, &c. &c. (See Schröckh, ib. 706.)

[1] To this Calixtus contributed theoretically by the sketch in the Apparatus Theologicus (in which there occurs an expression, very remarkable for those times, that " without the knowledge of ecclesiastical history, no theologian deserves the name," see the Epitome of the Fragment, in Schröckh, ib. 400-2.) and practically, by his own example in his different controversial works, which communicated itself to his scholars and disciples. (See Henke, ib. 255.) This historical character of the school, as far as its influence extended, weakened the dominion of formularism.

[2] His own Commentaries were indeed very imperfectly published, yet his Apparatus Theolog. shews at large the combined service of philology and philosophy in biblical interpretation; and Hackspan, one of the best commentators of the age, was his disciple.

[3] To this place belongs the controversy " whether good works were necessary to salvation," for maintaining which his colleague Horneius was termed Papist, Majorist, Anabaptist, and severely condemned by Wittenberg, Jena, and Leipzig. Calixtus, to avoid ambiguity or offence, employed other terms; yet because he urged as a motive to chastity, (in his Historia Josephi) that

F

pared the way for the exertions of Spener. Remarkable is it also, in proof of the ill effects of the existing controversies, that the persons, who in this century most promoted the advance of theological science, were either pupils of Calixtus, or of the same uncontentious disposition [1].

The present controversy was estimated by men of high talent [2] entirely unconnected with party;

salvation might be endangered by the contrary sins, this exhortation was converted into the position that chastity, (and thus good works,) were necessary to salvation, and the same imaginary heresies supposed to be involved. (Weism. ib. 1198, 9.)

[1] Among the former may be mentioned the celebrated Hackspan, Durr, (the first expander of the science of Christian moral) and the elder Fabricius; among the latter John Gerhard, (whom Bossuet calls " le troisième homme de la Reformation après Luther and Chemnice," Hist. des Var. T. 2, p. 455.) and to whom Du Pin preferred Melanchthon alone, (Biblioth. des Auteurs separés de la Comm. de l'Église Rom. T. ii. p. 74, sqq.) but who was frivolously depreciated by many Lutheran contemporaries, (Schröckh, ib. 443.; Budd. Isag. i. p. 353, sq.; Weism. ib. 1127.) Tarnov, Glassius, M. Geier, Sagittarius, Kortholt, S. Schmidt, Reuchlin; of the same spirit were the few, who presented striking exceptions to the decayed and lifeless system of preaching,—Arndt, J. V. Andreá, Herberger,—and of the learned theologians, J. Gerhard and Glassius. (See Schröckh, ib. 464—9; on J. V. Andreá there is a very interesting Memoir in Weism. ib. 1131—8.)

[2] These were the celebrated Glassius and Musæus. The opinion, which the former was commissioned by Ernest the Pious of Saxe Gotha to deliver on the points of controversy, was published after his death; and is " almost the only work (says Schröckh, 43. 250.) which furnishes a correct and moderate estimate of the controversy." Musæus, first in his lectures, estimated candidly the meaning of the expressions upon which the charges against the Calixtians were founded, (Weism. p. 1206.)

these virtually acquitted Calixtus; the only effect, however, of their candour was, to divert the contest in part against themselves; it was continued against the younger Calixtus, who possessed neither the talents, the learning, nor the temper of his father, and had degenerated into mere mutual revilings, before it sunk in the deeper interest of that with Spener and his followers.

Spener's endowments, (though he was possessed of considerable learning [1],) were rather of a moral and religious, than of a high intellectual nature.

and was consequently charged by a disciple of Calov with 93 errors in the most essential doctrines ; (Schröckh, ib. 251.) as those of Calixtus had varied from 80 to 120. (Schröckh, 39. 706.) These he refuted point by point, satisfactorily shewing their vexatiousness, and the danger which resulted to the Church from this wanton multiplication of controversy. (Weism. p. 1207.) Calov after Calixtus' death, refused to use the term " beatus C.," alleging that he must on the same ground speak of B. Bellarmine, B. Calvinus, B. Socinus, &c. (Weism. p. 1148.) and at Wittenberg, in a dramatic piece, Calixtus was represented as a fiend with horns and claws. (quoted by Henk. iv. 271.)

[1] Early intended for the pastoral office, he studied principally at Strasburg and Basle under Seb. Schmidt, (the best Scripture expositor of his time, and whose works are even now useful) Dennhauer and Buxtorf, Hebrew and other Oriental languages, history, and especially the interpretation of Scripture. His intimate study of Grotius' treatise De Bello et Pace, his being the author of the first considerable treatise on heraldry, (of which two editions were published,) and his delivery of lectures and holding disputations at Strasburg and Basle on geography and history, logic, and metaphysics, are indications of a more extensive knowledge not confined merely to actual theology. (see Schröckh, B. 43, S. 256. Canstein Leben Speners, §. 4, 5.) Still his best powers were given to theology, and much more to religion.

Even his sermons owed their attractions solely to their pure biblical and practical character. Those among his qualifications which approached most nearly to gifts of nature, a sound judgment[1], and a practical intuitive insight into the point upon which each question turned, were in him moral qualities. Through these endowments principally, combined with his own religious experience and his study of the history of the Church, he was enabled to see precisely what were the defects in its then state; his piety and religious zeal, supplied without pretension, in the regular performance of his functions, an example of the remedy for those defects. On these two points, then, turns the extensive, though from external circumstances still inadequate, reformation, which he was enabled to effect. He did not claim for himself the character of a reformer, and was perhaps on that very account, in those turbulent and intolerant times, the more calculated to be one. Too fully penetrated with the importance of the truths, whose neglect he deplored, in the slightest degree to compromise them for an unsound peace, yet was his manner of stating them conciliating and mild; confiding in the power of those truths, when stated, to make themselves acknowledged and felt, he withheld as much as possible his own individuality from mingling with them; he lived, as long as his opponents permitted him, for the discharge of his own duties alone,

---

[1] Leben Sp. S. 38, 9.

trusting that either the fruits of their right discharge might kindle others to like exertions, or that God would raise up others, who might carry into effect upon a more extensive scale that reform, whose necessity he proclaimed, but in which he himself was content to act a subordinate part. The alarm and jealousy were thus avoided, which might have resulted from bolder and more direct attempts. The princes of Germany valued and favoured him [1]. Enemies he had, from envy, from the unpalatableness of the truths which he promulgated, from his undervaluing the mere intellectual orthodoxism of his day, from his discovering that among the many things, on the laborious acquisition of which the orthodox theologians prided themselves, the one thing needful had been forgotten; but no one became Spener's enemy from any presumption or failing of his own. The following extract from a private letter [2] to a friend gives much insight into the Christian

---

[1] Witness his first unsolicited invitation to Dresden as first court preacher; and that subsequently to Berlin, when the displeasure of the Elector of Saxony at the earnestness of his preaching had emboldened his antagonists, and made his office painful; the confidence of the Elector of Brandenburg in entrusting to him all the theological appointments of the newly-erected University at Halle, (Schröckh, ib. 271.) and the invitation to resume his office at Dresden, (1698), at the very time that the divines of Saxony were declaiming against his deviations from the doctrines and constitution of the Evangelical Church. (Ibid. p. 282.)

[2] Published at Halle three years after his death, in the collection of his occasional writings and letters, entitled Theologische Bedenken, 32 Th. S. 305. (1708). This and the following extract are quoted by Schröckh, B. 43, S. 264.

mildness and humility of Spener's character, as well as into the principles upon which he acted. "To set myself up as a reformer of the Church were a folly, which I do not allow myself to entertain; I know sufficiently my own weakness, that I have received neither the wisdom nor strength for such a task. Let me then be contented to be numbered among the voices which encourage those to work a reformation, whom the Lord may have endowed with the ability thereto. For such a work then I need no followers, nor to draw others to me. Yet neither am I required to break with those Theologians, of whom I may either myself think and hope well, or who at least do not openly oppose the truth. Rather is it my aim to retain their good feelings in any way which is not contrary to my conscience; whether that their coinciding with me may make my own work succeed better, or that they may be thereby encouraged to a more diligent discharge of their office, or that they may not be seduced wickedly to oppose the Christian intentions of others. All which ends are in conformity with the glory of God. On the other hand I see not how it could be justifiable, wantonly to drive such needlessly to oppose themselves." Nor was this feeling of his own insufficiency momentary; it is expressed yet more fully, and therefore with more evident humility, in a letter to another friend, (1678)[1]. "I know well not only that the work of Reformation is not the work of one man,

---

[1] Schröckh, ib. S. 226.

but that, whatever may be the purpose of the Lord towards his Church, I shall neither be the chief agent, nor one of the chief; since he has not bestowed upon me the talents thereto. More honour already than I deserve is it that my God has so far blessed my " pia desideria," that they have sounded sufficiently loud to awaken and encourage many,—not to learn of me, but to reflect further on the subject according to the powers which they have from God." Of his inadequacy, which he here mentions in general terms, he assigns the grounds in another letter. " I find in myself a want of erudition and of natural qualifications, deficiencies which I observe in the execution of my functions, so that I am ashamed of being so little able to help myself. How then would it be, were I to undertake a thing so great? Especially am I deficient in the power of the Spirit from above, which is, alas! very weak; and my natural timidity even in small matters is difficult to overcome; nor can I do any thing which requires a truly heroic courage, but if the Lord of our Church design yet more to bless it, so that besides possessing true doctrine it should be brought generally into a sound condition, the agents must be very different from me and such as me." The agency of Spener, then, principally arose from the influence of his example, in the restoration of a more instructive and influential mode of preaching and of catechizing, and in the institution of those Unions for the promotion of piety and of Christian knowledge, which received the title of Collegia Pietatis; from his writings, and from the communication of the same spirit to others, especially to the Theologians of Halle.

The previous state of the pulpit has been already described. The evil was too universal to be felt. There was not light sufficient to make the darkness visible. Spener's reform commenced in the omission of the superfluous parade of dry learning, of unpractical controversy, of self-display, and of the cramped mechanism of the Arrangements. His preaching was a simple but energetic developement and application of the Gospel. It is indeed no slight proof of the dominion of controversy in preaching, that in one of his earliest sermons, (1667) ' on the necessary precautions against false prophets,' even he gave offence by including the Reformed among them [1]. The error was not repeated. Nor is the sensation excited by one, shortly subsequent, " on the false and insufficient righteousness of the Pharisees," in which he developed the incorrect ideas of many Christians on virtue and holiness, as if these consisted in the mere avoiding of gross vices, less a proof of the necessities of his times. Many there first learnt the insufficiency of unfruitful faith without amendment of the heart; some, unwilling to have their imagined security disturbed, refused again to enter his church [2]. Spener indeed did not cultivate one portion alone of the Christian system; he did not dwell exclusively on favourite doctrines, but

---

[1] Schröckh, ib. 262. Spener retained his regrets for this action even in his last sickness. (Leben S. 138.)

[2] Schröckh, l. c.

proposed the whole of Christianity. His three years' courses of sermons[1] contain severally, Gospel doctrine, Gospel duty, the consolations of Gospel faith. In the second especially, he taught not merely, as inexperienced moral teachers, *that* the duties were to be performed, but *how;* what facilitated, advanced, or hindered them[2]. Spener's anxiety to render belief practical is further evinced by his venturing to omit assertions, which were abused by fleshly-mindedness and indolence, but to the letter of which an indiscriminating Orthodoxy clung; such as that " No one can attain to the perfection which the divine law requires:" " in the act of justification, on the part of man, faith alone is concerned without good works," and by the revival of the often contested doctrine, that " good works are necessary to salvation[3]." It was, namely, one of Spener's main objects to remove the confidence in the dead faith, which the series of controversies had fostered[4]. The publication of these sermons, aided by Spener's living example, formed a new era in Christian preaching; the causes of the unfruitfulness of the former method became thus manifest: the

---

[1] They were published while Spener was at Dresden, 1688.
[2] Schuler, l. c. S. 22. fg. Allgemeine Biographie, Th. 6, S. 319. fg. 417, fg. ap. Schröckh, B. 43. S. 163.
[3] Mosheim, C. 17, P. 2, S. 2. c. 1. § 31. Not however that Spener held that justification was other than the free gift of God, but that good works as the fruits of faith were contained in it.
[4] See Löscher, one of Spener's bitterest antagonists, as quoted by Schröckh, B. 43, S. 289.

widest sphere however was opened to the pure biblical instruction of Spener, when theoretically as well as practically inculcated and exemplified by the first theologians of Halle, who united the offices of Professors and of Christian Ministers.

The defects of the catechetical system have been already noticed. Spener aimed at, and succeeded in, restoring the sense of its importance, which had been felt by every class even of the earliest Reformers[1], and had been earnestly inculcated by Luther, and in giving it a more instructive and practical character. The first he effected by undertaking its duties himself, when his high station in the Church did not make it a part of his office; (both as Senior of the Evangelical Ministerium at Frankfort, and as first court-preacher and member of the Upper Consistory at Dresden, whence in the latter office he could more effectually further it in others.) In both places he infused so much interest into his instructions, that even grown persons gladly availed themselves of them[2]. To the improvement of

---

[1] It is interesting and singular to see the practice independently revived by the Vaudois, by Wickliffe, and by Huss, after it had been nearly obliterated since the sixth century: (Budd. ib. 334, sqq.) and the circumstance adds to the proof, that Protestantism had its rise in the religious wants of Christians, not in intellectual difficulties, or in the much-praised scientific advancement of the age. Science aided indeed the Reformation, but was not its source; it can, and has as much perhaps assisted Romanism. Erasmus was more learned than any of the Reformers, yet was not himself one.

[2] Schröckh, ib. 151, fgg.

the mode of catechising he contributed principally by his " simple explanation of Christian doctrine according to the order of [Luther's] lesser catechism;" (1677.) a full and clear exposition of the sum of Christian faith, in reference to Christian life, with well-selected scriptural proofs [1]. His object in this work was to give a specimen how unpractised Christians might be taught, not by a mere mechanical exertion of the memory, but by developing their newly-acquired knowledge in their own language. He warned consequently against any mere adoption of his own model; he added tables, explanatory of his method, the more clearly to shew how little a mere adoption, or servile imitation, was necessary [2]. The science of catechetical instruction, which has since been expanded, owes its existence to this work of Spener's. Immediately connected with this improvement of elementary instruction was his revival of the rite of confirmation, whose solemnity and influence in the German Church now far exceeds that generally observable in our own; but which, until Spener, had sunk into neglect, as a supposed remnant of Popery [3].

Spener's widest influence, however, was derived from the institution of the much-questioned " collegia pietatis." The object of these at their first commencement, was to expand, explain, and apply the discourse of the preceding Sunday. He

[1] See Budd. ib. 336.
[2] Schröckh, ib.
[3] Henke, iv. 519.

had felt, in common probably with every practical minister, the inadequacy of any instruction, in which the people were mere recipients, either in imparting religious knowledge, or in giving an individual effect to what was delivered generally. In these meetings, which were commenced with prayer, part of the sermon was repeated, questions were asked by Spener to ascertain how far it had been understood, or proposed to him by any of the men present, not to satisfy curiosity, but to promote practical piety. These meetings continued to be conducted upon the same principles, when a passage of Scripture was laid as the basis instead of the sermon[1]. The free communication and the knowledge of the wants of the congregation re-acted upon the usefulness of the pulpit. These meetings were approved of by his colleagues, were in conformity with the symbolical books, praised by the Universities, and consulted even by Ben. Carpzov, who was subsequently, from envy, the great enemy[2] of Spener. In the Articles of Smalcald (III Th. Art. 4.) it is said,

[1] Schröckh, ib. S. 257.
[2] Carpzov's subsequent enmity arose in the disappointment of his expectation that the office at Dresden, which was given to Spener, should have been filled by himself or his brother. (Leben Sp. S. 118.) His brother actually was the successor of Spener. (Vater, 368.) This inconsistency, which Calovius shared with most of Spener's opponents, was excused by the idle distinction of a 'Spener prior et posterior,' though Spener continued to act uniformly to the end, and all his plans of reformation had been already developed. (Niemeyer die Universität Halle nach Ihrem Einfluss auf gelehrte u. prakt. Theol. S. 32.)

"Brotherly conferences out of the word of God, among the people, are a valuable aid to Christian advancement:" and B. Carpzov declared, with reference to these times, " The advantages of these meetings cannot be told, especially when the hearers thus communicate with their teachers; for unquestionably a common man learns more from one such meeting, than from ten sermons[1]." The example thus given speedily spread; similar meetings were instituted in other places, as Essen, Augsburg, Schweinfurt, Giessen, &c.; and though, in the place of their original institution, misrepresentation diminished their influence[2], in others they may have been inconsider-

[1] In his " Auserlesene Tugendspruche." Another passage is adduced by Lange Antibarb. T. 11. p. 171. " This wish of those enlightened and celebrated theologians, Dannhauer and Dorscheus, a zealous divine, (whom may God long continue to his Church) has not only very earnestly urged in his Pia Desideria, but has even shewn how Collegia Pietatis may be formed where there are no Universities, and laymen be admitted to speak in them. Whether they do well who despise them, and thwart them to the utmost of their power, when they might much promote them, time will shew." A similar opinion of Sagittarius is quoted by Weism. 1230, and others are mentioned generally.

[2] Schröckh l. c. mentions generally, that these meetings were removed twelve years afterwards, at the requisition of some ambassadors, into the Church, where the hearers having no longer the liberty of speaking, much of their usefulness of course fell away. In some places they were introduced without the superintendance of the minister, were naturally attended with irregularities, and suppressed under the name of conventicles. But these abuses were no necessary consequence of the institution, and Spener amply defended himself in a separate work, 1677, and in his

ately introduced, and were forbidden, yet they continued long a blessing to the Church, and were the means of recalling many, even of the learned, from the inventions and disputes of the schools, to the basis of a more fruitful theology, in piety and the study of the Scriptures [1]. On these were also founded the Collegia Biblica, which formed part of the widely-felt utility of the University of Halle.

Of Spener's writings many have already been occasionally mentioned. The most extensively useful were, perhaps, the Pia Desideria, and the works in vindication or explanation of it [2]. It is no slight proof of the mildness of Spener's character, that a production containing such bold,

"Allgemeine Gottesgelahrtheit," (Walch Einl. in d. Religions-Streitigk. 1 Th. S. 560, fg.) nor was he directly attacked on this head until after his death (by Löscher, Timotheus Verinus, 2 Th. S. 112. fg.)

[1] Twesten, p. 163. The University of Giessen, which in the later contests with the Pietists adopted the milder side against that of Rostock, seems to have long felt the influence of this earlier institution. Henke, Th. 8. S. 37.

[2] Buddeus bestows however great praise not only upon the writings mentioned, but upon his expositions of Scripture, especially one 'libellum plane aureum,' in which Spener collected and explained the passages of Scripture abused by worldly men to encourage a false security, (Isag. p. 1479.) and his "de natura et gratia," (on the difference of actions derived from man's natural powers, and those proceeding from the influence of the Holy Spirit,) "in which he was the first who abandoned the intricate, and often useless, questions of the schools, and made the enquiry throughout practical." (Ib. 592.) Lange says that even for the quickening of the natural intellect, there could be no better whetstone than Spener's writings. Anmm. zu. Sp. Leb. S. 38.

unwelcome, and sweeping truths, could have been so written, as to give so little offence, and to call forth at first universal approbation [1]. Spener received innumerable letters of thanks for this work; and not only the celebrated Kortholt, but even B. Carpzov, praised him for it. Yet Spener's censures extended to every branch of the Lutheran Church; he complained, that of the magistracy few knew what Christianity was; that, at the most, they only provided for the maintenance of the hereditary system; and that many hindered the good which religion might produce. That the order of the clergy required a thorough reform; that many lived in profligacy; many taught the letter only of Scripture; that numbers were such strangers to real earnest piety, that one zealous for it was looked upon as a Papist, Quaker, and Fanatic; that an immoderate value was attached to mere forms; that the clergy were looked upon as a caste of priests, like those of Rome, and wished to become so; that many deemed a mere peace from external enemies the most blessed condition of the Church, and therefore studied alone the means of subduing them, controversy. He dwelt also on the vices of the laity [2]. His proposed cure was extensive; his

---

[1] Henke, 3. 516. The testimonies of many of the most distinguished theologians were adduced by Spener himself, in a subsequent defence of Pietism, Gründl. Beantwortung des Unfugs der Pietisten, c. 1. § 15. fgg.

[2] Undoubtedly the whole of this lamentable state of the Church is not to be attributed to the contentious and unpractical theo-

views relating to the education of the clergy have been already named; on religious controversy especially, he timely warns, that right disputing about religion, even if free from irritation, is not sufficient, but must be accompanied with the apparent desire of improving the opponent, and of teaching him the wholesome application of the truth maintained [1]. Yet of all the positions in this work, two [2] alone, and these incidentally only

---

logy. The fearful excesses and the extremes of misery of the thirty years' war had demoralized and degraded Germany: still the state of religious teaching and religious education prevented the application of the remedy, which a better religious instruction might have afforded. No slight degree of misery fell upon Germany in the last desolating war; yet was the greater earnestness of mind, which this created, among the principal means of reviving religion; but unbelief is, for the most part, more reclaimable than a dead and contented orthodoxism.

[1] See the extract in Schröckh, ib. S. 289, fgg.

[2] These were, the one, Spener's favourite maxim, that " the theology of an unregenerate person was no real theology," but only a philosophising about divine things; which had been maintained, unquestioned, by his instructor, Dannhauer, and by many others. " Pietistica posthac sententia vocata est, et periculosus error," says Weismann, " quod mille forsan Theologi nostrates, tanquam gravem et arduam veritatem docuerunt." (Hist. Eccles. p. 1214, sq. where some authorities are quoted.) It was first opposed by Dielefield, a deacon in Nordhausen, 1679, and subsequently by the opposite assertion of Löscher, " that the ministry of an unconverted teacher was just as beneficial as if he were converted;" in support of which he appealed to the so-called gratia ministerialis, by which God was supposed uniformly to bless not only the administration of the Sacraments, " though administered by evil men," but their teaching also. With regard to the latter, Lange might well term this gratia ministerialis an

connected with its import, were at the time attacked, and the theologians of Saxony continued to praise his orthodoxy, until the displeasure of the Elector of Saxony, at his earnest, but strictly official [1], remonstrances, made opposition accept-

absurd and pernicious fiction. (See Spener Allg. Gottesgel. Fr. 1, 2. Löscher Timoth. Verimus, 1 Th. S. 281. fg. Pachomii Synops. Logom. Pietist. c. 1. qu. b. p. 5. ap. Schröckh, ib. p. 287, 8.) Yet Spener's maxim in other words, that no real theology can be conceived without piety and religious interest, no one would now think of questioning. Then, however, it was found to contain Pelagianism, Arminianism, Calvinism, Socinianism, &c. (see ap. Weism. ibid.) The other point related to the anticipation of better times, when Romanism having sunk, and the Jews having been converted, Christianity should attain a fuller and more glorious development; these cheering expectations Spener distinctly separated from the millenniary dreams of apocalyptic writers; he expected no earthly, no distinct kingdom, no kingdom of glory, which should replace the kingdom of grace; none, which should endure a precise period of ten centuries; but according to the analogy of the history of religion, and of Christianity itself, he did anticipate, that after the long contest which it has carried on, and in which it has been gaining successive victories, its conquest should be yet more manifest, that according to the prophets, a time should come " when the knowledge of the Lord should cover the earth, as the waters cover the sea." (See Spener's Behauptung der Hoffnung besserer Zeiten, 1693; his Vindication, 97; his Letzte Theologische Bedenken, 3 Th. S. 73; Löscher's Timoth. Ver. 1. Th. c. 1. and others ap. Schröckh, ib. S. 291, 2. Spener's Leben, S. 137.) Yet among a large portion of Spener's opponents, these hopes were deemed no better than the grossest conceptions of Chiliastic fanatics, were thought to overthrow the foundations of the faith, and the whole sum of Christian doctrine; to lead to seditions and tumults, &c. &c. (Weism, 1225.)

[1] Spener was his Confessor. Weism. p. 1168, says, Summam

able. From that date much of Spener's time was consumed in self-defence. Not only B. Carpzov then wrote against him, but the University of Wittenberg maintained its character by setting forth two hundred and sixty-four errors which were to be found in his writings; twenty-five of these relate to the symbolical books [1]; of the rest

prudentiam, modestiam, gradationemque scrupulosissimam in sacro suo officio in Aula gerendo observavit B. Spenerus, at ne sic quidem causam, non suam, sed Dei, perficere potuit.

[1] The allegations against Spener with regard to the symbolical books, as far as they were allegations, have been justly reckoned by Zeltner among the Anti-pietistic Logomachies, (under the name of Pachomius, Synopsis Logomach. ut vulgo vocant Pietisticarum, a. 59. 72, fg.) Spener acknowledged that these books contained divine truths, he believed them free from errors in doctrine, yet he justly thought that confusion and symbololatry alone could arise from terming them " inspired," (as comprising doctrine originally given by inspiration) which his opponents required of him. (Weism. ib. 1226, fg. Budd. ib. 474, fg. Schröckh, ib. 191, fgg.) In the much agitated question of the use of the quia or the quatenus in the subscription of the symbolical books, which Spener did not originate, but which he was called upon to decide, he wished only that those, who for conscience sake declined the apparently stricter formula, might be allowed to employ the " quatenus;" yet he himself always used the former. Indeed the two formulæ mutually imply each other; no conscientious man could subscribe to articles, " so far as they agreed with Holy Scripture," who did not believe that in their principles, that in all essentials, they did so agree; nor can it be thought that every individual, who subscribes them " because they so agree," necessarily binds himself to every incidental expression, so that he agree in the principle. As to the value of the symbolical books, Spener said, that " none held them in greater respect, treated and *inculcated* them on their hearers with greater diligence than those who were reproached as Pietists, and

many illustrate the character of the orthodoxism of that period; it was deemed erroneous then, that he considered a holy life as absolutely necessary, since without it no one could have a true faith; that the truth and sincerity of the repentance was indispensable to the validity of absolution; that in all absolution a condition was implied; that the intention to reform was a preparation for repentance; that all revenge was forbidden; that the Scripture was no power of God, so long as it was neither read nor heard; that the Greek of the New Testament was, in different books, more or less elegant, the Holy Spirit having conformed himself to the style of each writer [1]; that Holy Scripture was then only a source of religious knowledge, when it was understood according to the meaning of the Holy Spirit; that ministers were mere guides to the real teacher, the Holy Spi-

---

that the whole question was not about the real value, use, estimation, or authority of the symbolical books, but about their abuse by certain Theologians to charge heresy upon unmeriting and orthodox men." (ap. Weism. 1227.) Neither did his followers diminish the respect attached to them. (Schröckh, ib. 193.) The neglect of the symbolical books was the effect, not the cause of change in doctrine.

[1] This extraordinary hypothesis, which, in a manner readmitted human individuality in the composition of the Scripture, at the same time that it denied it, became predominant, when the difference of style and of the purity of the language in the different books had been put beyond question by the progress of criticism; in Spener's time the admission itself was thought to derogate from inspiration.

rit, and Christ in him; that believers are, in matters of belief, free from all human authority; that heretics, out of that Church, might possess faith, real love, the Holy Spirit, and eternal happiness; that much might be learnt and imitated from the Reformed, the Romanists, the Anabaptists, Quakers, and other parties; that the new man was not less nourished by the bread and wine in the Lord's Supper, than the natural man by the natural bread and wine, &c. &c [1].

Yet notwithstanding the vindications of himself thus extorted, in which, however, Spener still manifested the same practical and conciliating spirit, his indefatigable industry enabled him to maintain an almost incredibly large correspondence on all the subjects which mainly occupied his long life, manifesting a very deep acquaintance with the necessities of the Church, and a sound judgment on the means of meeting them. Through these he exerted no merely temporary influence over a large portion of the German

[1] The title is curious: " Christ-Luthrische Vorstellung in deutlichen aufrichtigen Lehrsätzen, nach Gottes Wort und d. Symbol. Kirchenbüchern, sonderlich d. Augsb. Conf., und unrichtigen Gegensätzen aus Hrn Spener's Schriften, zur Ehre des grossen Gottes, Erhaltung der Göttlichen Wahrheit, auch Beylage der Augsb. Conf. u. d. and. symbol. Bücher, geistlichen Vereinbarung d. aufrichtigen Theologen, treuer Warnung der rechtgläubigen Lutheraner, u. s. w. aufgesetzt u. publicirt von den Theologis in Wittenberg." Well might a theologian of those days say with a sigh, " in more nunc positum esse apud multos, ut lubentius centum hæreticos, quam unum faciant Christianum." (ap. Weism. 1215.)

Church. Four quarto volumes were published in his life, besides those which were subsequently collected[1]. At Berlin, also, as well at Dresden, he maintained in his own family and formed many, who continued to act after his death in the same principles.

Spener, then, both by his direct improvements, by his revival of Biblical enquiry and historical investigation, by his concessions that other communions might in some respects be more correct than the Lutheran, by his disapprobation of some rites in his own Church[2], by the admission that though it was clear from fundamental errors, it, as little as any other Church, could be free from

---

[1] The principal subjects of this collection were, the best method of Theological learning; Christian doctrine and moral, especially the promotion of piety; the explanation of Biblical passages; cases of difficulty in the Christian ministry; the necessary improvements in the Church, and the safest mode of their execution; Ecclesiastical law; the general and particular state of the Church; Christian principles of conduct towards Christians of a different persuasion; judgments on a great number of remarkable men and their opinions; " a treasure of practical observations, and admonitions, for Theologians, Ministers, and Christians, of many ranks." (Allgem. Biogr. 6ter Th. S. 444, fg. ap. Schr. ib. S. 130.)

[2] Of Confession, for example, as it then existed, (Letzte Theol. Bedenken, 3 Th. S. 723.) he says that " almost all conscientious preachers looked upon it as a burthen, and that he himself was glad from his heart that he had now nothing to do with it." Exorcism at Baptism he termed an useless ceremony, which might easily prove cause of offence, and might well be abolished. (Theol. Bed. 1 Th. S. 157, fg.)

all[1], and by the spirit of enquiry to which these principles gave rise, shook, incidentally, the supposed infallibility and perfection, which was virtually ascribed to the old system, and upon which its security rested. His immediate followers carried on practically the improvements whose theory he had given, and through the erection of the University of Halle obtained an extensive and influential field of action.

The bitter polemics of the Lutherans of Wittenberg[2], (whither the Prussian students, and especially those of the Mark, had for the most part been wont to repair) suggested to the Elector of Brandenburg, who wished for concord, the erection of an University, nearer, and more peaceful. Halle was already a place of education, and was adopted at the recommendation of Thomasius, who had withdrawn thither, having been removed from Leipzig by the persecutions of the orthodox Theologians[3]. The three who at first composed the Theological faculty there, Francke, Anton, and Breithaupt, had all more or less, derived their spirit from Spener; Anton and Breit-

---

[1] Theol. Bed. 3 Th. S. 706, fg.

[2] Above thirty years before, Fred. Will. the Great had been obliged, on the same grounds, to refuse to prefer any Theological students educated at Wittenberg. (Henke, iv. 279.)

[3] These were excited by his defence of Francke, and his justification of intermarriage between the Lutheran and the Reformed, in the course of which he gave offence to Casp. Löscher of Wittenberg, who procured his removal. (Henke, iv. 542, fg.)

haupt had been formed by him at Frankfort; the zeal of Francke for the promotion of piety had been furthered, and its character determined, by a two month's residence with him at Dresden. Immediately upon his return, he, as a subsidiary teacher (privatim docens) at Leipzig, as well as Anton, had held Biblical lectures, and presided at the meetings of the students for the study of Scripture [1]. These were continued for some months unnoticed; the numbers mounted to some hundreds; many of the hearers became distinguished for the exemplariness of their life; and though some may not have been free from peculiarities, an investigation instituted in consequence of calumny, fully acquitted them of misconduct [2]. The University reported the blamelessness of the lectures, yet Francke was suspended, though Thomasius, and Sagittarius, entirely unconnected with him, wrote in his defence. The meetings were continued by Schade, and severer measures followed [3]; Pietism, as it was then first called, was

[1] The Magistri were allowed in the feriæ caniculares to read theological lectures. (Kanst. ebend. S. 119.)

[2] The principal accusations against Francke were, that he had spoken against philosophy and disputation, and had maintained that the Christian's happiness began on earth; those against the students, that they had burnt their abstracts of the lectures, spoken ill of polemic, &c.

[3] The so-called Pietistic students were deprived of their pensions; any one who attended one of these meetings was refused his testimonials, excluded from any office, &c. yet the Leipzig Protocol names nothing fanatical which had taken place in them. It must be observed, that the name of Pietists was not assumed by themselves, but given to them, sneeringly, by

forbidden, and a harsh contest carried on, principally by Carpzov, until the erection of the new University allowed the reform to be pursued undisturbed, though not unopposed [1].

The free circulation of talent or merit, which has ever taken place through every part of Germany, independent of the accident of the spot of its first formation, gave more importance to the new institution, than would, perhaps, in this country be generally conceived. Halle became, like Geneva of old, the heart from which the impulse of the new principles became felt in every part of the system. In the first thirty years of its institution, 6034 Theologians had been admitted into it, besides the thousands which were educated at the numerous schools supported in the Orphan-House founded [2] by Francke. An

their opponents, who themselves took that of the Orthodox. (Schröckh. 43. 272.)

[1] The next year, (1795), produced the Wittenberg Manifesto against Spener; and Carpzov, in a second Programm which he wrote against him, did not hesitate to term this mild and peaceful man a procellam ecclesiæ, tempestatem pacis, turbonem religionis, nay, a Spinozist. The irritation against Spener did not cease even with his death; it was a question at different Universities whether the term "beatus Spener" could be used. Professor Fecht, of Rostock, published a work, "De beatitudine mortuorum in Domino," in which he decides that this could be said of the extremely impious, who die without any external mark of repentance; of all sinners but those who die in the commission of gross sin (Par. 18.) but not of Spener. (See at length in Kanstein's Leben. S. 109—117.) Others, who decided similarly, are mentioned generally by Weism. 1168; the contrary was even declared sinful. Niemeyer, ib. S. 32.

[2] This establishment, which was commenced by Francke, in

institution, which collaterally perfected, by the opportunities which it afforded for catechetical instruction, the practical character of the ministers educated at Halle[1]. The usefulness of these preparations was further promoted by the establishment of Kanstein, a disciple of Spener, for the printing of Bibles, (by which much more than two millions of Bibles, and a million of Testaments have been circulated), and that for the printing of Christian writings and for the cheaper sale of books of education.

The plan pursued at Halle was conducted by its first founders on the principles of Spener, the same as those of the earlier Reformation; a recurrence from human forms and human systems to the pure source of faith in Scripture; a substitution of practical religion for scholastic subtleties and unfruitful speculation. On these two points then, the promotion of scriptural study and of the practical direction of the several theological sciences, turns the peculiar method of the instruction of Halle. Scripture interpretation again

---

1697, with seven gulden (14 sh.) so much increased before his death, that 600 children were supported daily, 2000 instructed, 120 teachers maintained. It was a pattern for many others, and a nursery for instructors in the schools of every class (Henke, iv. 548, fg.) Yet even this institution did not escape the censure of the orthodox party; e. g. V. E. Löscher Unsch. Nachr. and Meyer. (ap. Henke, ib.) The Danish Missionary Institution was subsequently erected there, and the interest in the extension of the Gospel abroad was influential, as it always is, in promoting its domestic progress.

[1] Niemeyer, ib. S. 53. fg.

became as among the first Reformers, the root of theological study. It was theoretically promoted by the lectures[1] of the highly-gifted and learned Francke, on the " Principles of Interpretation," which tended, at least negatively, to free it from the subserviency to doctrinal systems, both by their own extensive immediate influence, and as the foundation of the work of Rambach, which was nearly exclusively employed for almost half a century[2]. Though the principle of the analogy of faith was still held as the basis of right interpretation, its abuses were in some measure checked both by positive restrictions, and by the simplification of the system itself; and though on the other side the predominantly practical character may, by directing the search to a higher spiritual meaning beyond that of the letter, have ministered occasion to subsequent arbitrariness, yet Francke does not seem to have intended more than the acknowledged and important truth, that a deeper and more spiritual study will ever find a deeper truth in Scripture, or than the legitimate employment of analogical application. With this theory of biblical exposition, were united lectures on all the principal parts of the Bible, embracing principally the practical side; a course not to be judged of according to the usual character of practical commentaries, in which

[1] The Manuductio ad lectionem Script. Sacræ, frequently reprinted in German and Latin, and in the latter language even in England.
[2] Schröckh, 42. 614.

the topics dwelt upon are rather united with, than deduced from the text. Independent study of Scripture was further encouraged by the successive correction of passages in Luther's version, (remarkable as the first published[1] attempt in the same language), an attempt which, in Francke, can only indicate anxiety[2] for their better understanding, and freedom from the prevailing timidity, which an adherence to system had engendered. Of lasting service, finally, for the extension of Biblical knowledge, were the Collegium Orientale Theologicum, and the Seminarium Ministrorum Ecclesiæ, of which the former, besides promoting the study of the languages connected with the Old Testament, and giving rise to the first critical edition of the Hebrew Bible[3], contributed to the propagation of

[1] That which the learned Saubert commenced at the command of August, Duke of Brunswick, 1665, was broken off in the midst of 1 Sam. 17, at the death of the Duke, and even the published part suppressed (Schröckh 42, 598, Henke, 3, 285, fg.) so completely, that Buddeus, ib. p. 112, supposes it never to have been published. Calov and others raised a clamour against it before they had seen it, and its continuation was probably prevented by the influence of one of the polemic preachers removed from Brandenburg.

[2] It gave rise, however, to bitter invectives against Francke, from Meyer, Beck, and others of the orthodox party. Meyer entitles one of his, " a warning to students not to be led astray by Francke's work;" in another he calls this work " a temptation of Satan, by which he endeavours to cast into yet worse confusion the on every side persecuted Church." See on the controversy Budd. p. 1360, sqq. Walch Religions-streitigk. 1 Th. S. 731, fg.

[3] That of J. H. Michaelis, completed by the assistance of

Christianity among the Jews and Mohammedans[1]. The same practical character was given by Breithaupt and Freylinghausen to doctrinal studies; after the example of Spener, all scholastic, and even unbiblical terminology, except what was admitted by the universal church, was excluded, and the long-forgotten element of Christian experience was by the former restored[2]. In moral theology, though as yet little cultivated as a science, the declarations of this school in the Adiaphoristic controversy, that no action was to the individual who performed it indifferent, evinced a deeper insight into the principles of Christian action[3]. Polemic again was taught by

Breithaupt and Anton, (Vater S. 366), which is even now of use; the same institution also gave birth to the valuable work of J. H. and C. B. Michaelis on the Hagiographa.

[1] See J. L. Schulze in Francken's Stiftungen, B. I. S. 209, ap. Vat. S. 365.

[2] Freylinghausen in the Grundlegung der Theologie, Budd. p. 362; on Breithaupt's Instit. Theol. see Budd. p. 361. and 390.

[3] On this as on every other occasion, in which this controversy has been renewed, both parties appear to have forgotten the principle which seems to lie in the precepts of St. Paul, that, though nothing is indifferent to individuals, many things are so, except to individuals; the character of the action depending entirely upon the influence which it exerts upon the mind of the person performing it, some of them may have more *tendency* than others to produce an ill effect, and thus lose to a certain degree the character of ἀδιάφορα, yet none but the individual himself can know whether they have that effect, and therefore though a minister may warn of their *tendency*, they must still in each case remain matters of private judgment. In the present case, however, not merely the usual topics of this controversy, but the pleasures of the appetite, the desire of honor, glory, riches,

Anton, according to the beautiful view of Spener, in which every real heresy was considered as it originated in moral defects; the heretic was regarded as one labouring under a disease; the teacher recollected, that though exempt from this, he was not free from other diseases, and endeavoured to restore him as a friend, not to harass him as an antagonist. The greatest change, however, was in the science, whose better cultivation was one great object of all these, pastoral theology: the defects of the former century had, in the orthodox school, become confirmed in the commencement of this; what was then custom, had now become law; the train of grammatical, historical, polemical, expositions of the text, was now fixed in the elementary treatises; they varied only, in that now the fivefold practical application consisted in the polemic against the pietists. The style was full of the same pedantic display and unnatural conceits; and as if to prevent the possibility of free-exertion of mind, the artificial plans of arranging the discourse were now invariably determined; and ingenuity and strength were wasted and perverted in arranging the same text according to the greatest variety of methods[1]. The practical character of the whole

and pre-eminence, were placed by the orthodox party among things indifferent. see Weism. p. 1250.

[1] These were swelled by the often-mentioned J. B. Carpzov to 100; some of them were named from the mode of treating the text, some from the inventor, some from the university where they were the most used, e. g. Leipzig, Helmstadt, Königsberg,

theology of Halle must necessarily introduce better principles; method, style, and illustration were no longer valued for themselves, but as means; a right and faithful application of Scriptural Interpretation, Doctrinal Theology, and Christian moral to catechetic and pulpit instructions, were a main object of the Collegia Biblica; the previous system, whose defects originated in an entire misconception of the preacher's office, fell at once [1] among those who became acquainted with a more living Christianity; that, by which it was replaced, was guarded against its natural deflection, a neglect of all rules, by the scientific developement of Lange and Rambach [2], as it was

Wittenberg, (Schuler, 1 Th. S. 180, fg.; 2 Th. S. 8, fg. ap. Schröckh, 43, 160-1.) To apply 50 of these plans to a single text was considered a meritorious performance; Löscher indeed, according to Schröckh, reduced them to 25, but " those he retained were in their execution not much better than the rest," (Id. ibid.)

[1] The vain display of pedantic learning seems to have been among the most deeply rooted evils; against this Francke and Freylinghausen, (both distinguished preachers, and the latter considered as the best model of his age, see Knapp, Francken's Stiftungen, 2 B. S. 305.) opposed the principle of Luther, who " in Wittenberg did not preach to the 40 doctors or magistri who might be there, but to the crowd of young people, children, and populace."—" To them," added Luther, " I preach; to them I conform myself; according to their wants I speak; if the rest like it not thus simply, the door stands open." Francke in his lectures refers to the example of our Saviour, who had indeed in the Pharisees learned hearers, yet told them in what they were wanting, in terms as simple as could be used.

[2] Rambach was one of the most active and efficient disciples of the school of Halle; though not possessed of an original mind, nor

practically realized in the preaching of Francke and Freylinghausen. Two apparently slight innovations, the alternation of continuous explanations of large portions of Scripture[1] with the usual synthetic preaching, and the occasional selection of passages not contained in the appointed sections of the Church, as subjects of the discourses, are too obvious improvements to have been noticed, but that the general adherence to all the defects of the hereditary system implies the more decided practical character in those who perceived them. The doubt of the sufficiency of these pericopæ, which had been continued as they had existed in Germany previous to the

able to strike out new views, he has well embodied in a scientific form the practical principles of his school. He was widely influential in his life at Halle, Jena, and Giessen, and was referred to even by Mosheim as the best model for general preaching. (Schröckh, ib. 170.) His Wohlunterrichteter Catechet, 1722, and his Erläuterung über die Præcepta homiletica, a posthumous work, were long the best and favourite treatises in each department. Lange's work was the Oratoria Sacra ab artis homileticæ vanitate repurgata.

[1] The advantages of this species of lecture, alternating with discourses on set subjects, are sufficiently obvious, and have been witnessed by the author in Germany; the most fruitful source of mistakes in doctrine, the interpretation of texts independent of and contrary to the context, to which so great occasion is given by the division into verses, is thereby, and thereby alone can it be, checked; the understanding of Scripture in private study is materially facilitated; the habit of investigating its meaning, and of considering its varied references, is substituted for a mere perusal of its letter; the instruction conveyed is more easily recollected, being as it were incorporated with the passage explained.

Reformation[1], but which both limited the knowledge of Scripture, and the subjects of the discourses, and interfered with the natural connection and the order of these subjects, was received as a mark of alienation from the Lutheran Church[2]. Spener's principles of catechising, (the Socratic method) again were expanded by Rambach, and the readiness acquired in the practice of the Orphan-house added to the superiority to the teachers of Halle. This practical theological tendency was furthered by private intercourse of a corresponding character; at regularly recurring seasons of the week, the character of a theologian, as a servant of the Church, the necessity of not forgetting the one thing needful amid the earnestness of intellectual study, was illustrated and impressed; the circumstances promoting or advancing right theological study were discussed; the scientific and practical elements were blended in the Collegia Biblica; other meetings were held, in which the professors were consulted as fathers; so that most students were known personally to them; theologians of evil lives were recommended to embrace some other profession.

[1] Budd. Isag. 1343, 1412, 1426, sq. some evils attending them are briefly alluded to, ib. 1430.
[2] E. g. in Löscher's diss. Anticalviniana de pericopis Evang. et Apostol. The pericopæ for the morning service being mostly taken from the Gospels, and a large proportion being accounts of miracles, the subjects of Christian instruction must, where there was no evening lecture, if the pericopa be adhered to, be either omitted, or very artificially connected with the text.

The influence of this system was, for a time, felt not in Germany alone, but in Denmark, in Sweden, even in Greece, in mount Athos; teachers of youth, and ministers were sought from Halle, in every part of Germany[1]; others were kindled by their example, and the plans of benevolence as well as the piety of Halle were extended in the places, whither they were invited[2]. The bodies, thus organized, long continued to exist, and indeed never wholly lost their influence, though the master-movement, which had first given them impulse, slackened, and in great measure ceased, with the death of Francke, and the first founders of the school. The same spirit more or less influenced C. B. Michaelis, the younger Francke, Freilinghausen, the elder Knapp, (" cujus vita," says his biographer Nösselt[3], " commentatio æternitatis fuit;") Callenberg, (the pious founder of the institutions for

---

[1] Niemeyer, l. c. S. 53.
[2] Vid. inter al. Niemeyer, l. c. S. 58.
[3] Sammlung Nösseltsch. Aufsatz. von Niemeyer, S. 192, where the character of this perfect Christian is at large described. The separation, however, of the theoretical and practical side of Theology had already commenced, and diminished the influence of G. Francke, Knapp, and Callenberg. (On the two last see Semler's Lebensbeschreibung, 1 Th. S. 87. fgg.) The unaffected and pure piety of Knapp obtained him veneration even from those, whose scientific requisitions he did not satisfy; yet, though he possessed respectable learning, his influence appears, even in the account of Nösselt, to have been principally practical. On Francke and Callenberg, see also Niemeyer, der Univ. Halle, S. 72. fg.

H

the conversion of Jews and Mohammedans,) and Baumgarten. Yet in part the times themselves were altered; a too predominant cultivation of the mere understanding had commenced even in the latter days of Francke, as himself complains [1]; the antagonists against whom the school had to contend, were differently and more scientifically formed; in part also the system itself was liable to misrepresentation, in part exposed actually to suffer both from scientific and moral degeneracy. Of the liability to mis-statement, their Pseudo-Lutheran opponents had fully availed themselves. Not only had they excited popular violence [2], and obtained the interposition of civil interference to suppress the " schools of piety [3];" but had dili-

[1] In a lecture, 1709, upon the difference of the present and former students of Theology.

[2] As in the tumults at Hamburg, where Meyer (formerly Professor at Wittenberg,) irritated by Spener's official remonstrances on his life, having first attempted to impose a new formula of subscription upon Spener's brother-in-law, Horbius, preached against him as a lying prophet and priest of Baal; so that Horbius having once escaped at the risk of life, was obliged to leave the city by night. See Vater, 360. Henke, iv. 525. fgg.

[3] Henke gives, from Walch's Religionsstreit. and the Pantheon Anabaptistar. et enthusiast., the following list of places where edicts were published against the Pietists: Wolfenbüttel, (1692); Gotha, (1697); Zelle, (1698); Hannover, (1703); Bremen, (1705); Stutgard, (1706); Nürnberg, (1707); Zerbst, (1709); Hannover again, (1710 and 1711); Berlin, (1711); and says that the list, in Germany, might easily be increased. It was also proscribed in Sweden and Denmark; (Henk. S. 528.) in Wolfenbüttel even some clergy were forbidden to meet to read the Scripture together, and, on refusal to comply, were removed to lower stations; in Erfurt

CHARACTER OF THEOLOGY IN GERMANY. 99

gently confounded their tenets, principles, and objects with those of the wildest and most disgraceful fanatics, whose appearance always tarnishes and obstructs, and seems indeed an evil almost inseparable from, any great and sudden revival of religion. It were scarcely credible, but for the knowledge that every fanatical sect was classed, with Wickliffe, under the same title of Lollard, and that Luther had some difficulty in separating his cause from that of the Anabaptists, that the immediate and pure followers of Spener should have been identified by their opponents with the most wretched and abandoned fanatics of their times, that the degrading excesses of the deeply-sunken view of Butler [1] should have been deprecated under the title of Pietism. Old and new titles of heresies were put in requisition to stigmatize the school of Halle; Pelagianism, Socinianism, Jesuitism, Schwenkfeldianism, Osiandrism, were, with many others, found [2] united

---

all meetings to read the Bible were forbidden under penalty of a fine of 15*l.*; and when Sagittarius, writing in defence of Francke, asserted that Pietism was only a living Christianity, the Elector of Saxony wrote to the Duke of Weimar to inform him of, and to request him duly to punish, his unquiet Professor Theologiæ.

[1] This was done by the above-named Meyer, then Gen. Superintendant in Pomerania; and Breithaupt and Francke were compelled to disclaim all connection with these miscreants. (Walch, Th. 11. S. 769. ap. Vat. 367. Henke, 8. 40, 41.) They answered, that the faculty of Halle had nothing to do with those called Pietists in that report, but that it were "better that the name were altogether omitted."

[2] Henke quotes (iv. 520, 521) the following titles of treatises

in their principles; and though, following the example of Spener [1], they earnestly opposed themselves to every manifestation of a schismatical spirit, they were invariably charged with a Pharisaical separatism. More dangerous, however, than external violence, were the liabilities to degeneracy in the system itself. The abuse lay so close to the use, the means employed were in such close

---

against the Pietists. *Meyer* de Pietistis veteris ecclesiæ—de Socinianismo Pietistarum—de fraternitate P. et Jesuitarum—*Loescher* de Schwenkfeldianismo in Pietismo renato—*Edzardi* Machiavellus Pietisticus.—*Bücher* Rathmanna redivivus.—*Fecht* de Pelagianismo a Lutheranor. doctrina depulso—epistolæ antipraedestianæ.—*Wernsdoff* Osiandrismus in Pietismo redivivus, &c. According to the definition of Schelwig, another opponent, " Pietism is a sect, instituted and promoted by Spener, of Anabaptists, Schwenkfeldians, Weigelians, Rathmannians, Labadists, Quakers, and other fanatics, (under the pretence of a new Reformation and of the hope of better times) for the harassing and final destruction of the Church attached to the Augsburg Confession, and the other symbolical books." Weism. ib. 1211.

[1] Spener uniformly and earnestly set himself against the Pharisaical separation, which occasionally manifested itself, even in the earlier period of his ministry. (Schröckh, 43. 265.) His principles may be partly collected from the extracts already given, partly from his, " der Klagen üb. d. verdorbene Christenthum Missbrauch u. rechter Gebrauch." Frft. 1684, 1696, (cp his Theol. Bedenk. Th. 1. S. 634. Consil. P. iii. S. 517.) Towards the end of his life, Spener equally opposed the too general declamations of Schade against the Confessional as tending to produce divisions. It were easy to multiply instances or authorities; suffice the brief statement of the ecclesiastical historian; " Never did Spener, or any of his genuine disciples, favour separatism in the Church." (Schr. ib. 285.)

connection with principles, where self-deception is most easy and most dangerous, they required for their exertion the combination of such varied gifts; (not deep piety alone, but sound judgment, and extensive knowledge of human nature,) that decay and abuse were much to be apprehended, as soon as the comprehensive mind, which first set them in action, was withdrawn. All religious forms, and especially those expressive of religious feeling, have a tendency to lose the spirit by which they were originally animated; this may again be revived, but in the mean-time the employment of the form alone, whose significance is either insensibly changed or wholly lost, produces in those who use it, a more or less conscious hypocrisy. The whole history of the Church furnishes the proof, that every new strong awakening of religious feeling brings with it a peculiar form of expressing that feeling; it gives, too, the painful confirmation, that in all cases the form has been continued, when the spirit, which produced it, is departed. The same phenomenon is found in individuals as well as in classes; the language of early days is frequently retained, while the feeling, which produced that language, exists only in reminiscence of those times. This aberration is the more injurious, in that, while the conscious hypocrisy generally invests itself in the mere external peculiarities or practices, which in the first instance arose from religious principle, the comparatively, and often almost wholly, unconscious consists in the adherence to the language which originally expressed deep religious feeling, or for which either other ideas are imperceptibly substituted, or those before entertained are, for a time alone, renewed. The temporary feeling, excited by the recurrence to these forms, induces or facilitates, self-deception; the use of the forms, destitute of their spirit, deadens, yet further, that spirit in the individual. The form, in which the re-awakened Christianity exhibited itself in the time of Spener, may be considered in contrast with the subsequent deflections, under the heads of the language and actions, in which it expressed itself, and of the means of its preservation or extension. In none of these are the first founders of the Pietistic school open to censure. The religious language of Spener and Francke possesses all the copiousness, and purity, and life, natural to minds deeply penetrated by their subject, imbued with the treasures of Scripture, and sufficiently enlarged to reject no expressions, by whomsoever they might have been before used, which furnished a pure vehicle of Christian sentiment and Christian devotion. The unpractical formulæ of the school alone were set aside, other language, whether of the orthodox or the mystics, but especially from the pure and rich fountain of Luther, was, under this single limitation, equally admitted; and the deadening effects of uniform or systematic expression were thus obviated. The later Pietists contracted, instead of expanding and perpetuating, this system; on the one hand they limited their riches by a too hasty rejection of much of the moral language of the orthodox school, as well as of the expressions of the Moravians, who had arisen from among them; on the other, the original freshness of the stamp of their own was worn away, and what had once conveyed the " free spirit" of Spener became as technical and lifeless as the phraseology of the orthodox, to which it had been opposed, and more pernicious, from the very depth of its original significance. A mere vague and general meaning was attached to what had originally conveyed definite Christian ideas. II. The means adopted to preserve and extend this spirit were, as above stated, meetings for the practical study of Scripture, for mutual consultation and assistance, and more than ordinary domestic and public devotion. The strongest hold of formalism is in the very means employed to promote devotion: great watchfulness is requisite against self-deception, from considering them as more than means; great discrimination in the recommendation of these means to others. In both, lamentable mistakes were committed by the later members of this school; hypocrisy was engendered by the too great stress laid upon private edifying and Christian conversation; their indiscriminate[1]

---

[1] This indiscriminateness manifested itself in the anxiety to induce all the students, on their entering the University, to participate in all these meetings, without regard to the stage of Christianity in which each might then be; and in the ill estimation in which those were held, who omitted them when interfering with their studies. The failure to perceive that these

and too frequent employment, where the mind was yet unprepared to profit by them, the use of "strong meat" where "milk" alone could nourish, produced, often, re-action and disgust; in other cases religious conversation was engaged in as a mere act of duty, and as a test of religion; and the probably but half-conscious, hypocrisy, which employed the expressions, without a corresponding feeling, of religion, deadened the heart. III. The actions, finally, in which the religious spirit manifested itself were in part only liable to perversion; neither the zeal for plans of benevolence, nor the resignation of expensive gratifications to promote them, which distinguished the school of Halle, nor the highly-prospered efforts to extend Christianity among the heathen, were well susceptible of it. The degree of value, however, attached to the abstinence from amusements, whose character is derived solely from their influence upon each individual, (the so-called ἀδιαφορα,) became a source both of self-deception and of breaches of Christian charity; a deflection,

---

meetings were for that, and for most ages, too crowded, seems scarcely credible. On the Sunday there were, one with the citizens, two in the afternoon with the Professors, (also purely practical,) one in the family in the evening, each lasting an hour, besides the three times attending divine service. Much of the character of the later system of Halle, and of its incidental disadvantages, may be collected from Semler's autobiography; from this it appears, that when the attendance at these meetings began to be valued for its own sake, the perfect rectitude of the means employed to induce attendance was not always regarded.

invariably occurring, as soon as the abstinence is regarded as being in itself a Christian duty. A legal yoke is then substituted for Christian freedom; and things, in the first instance acknowledged by the party itself to be of subordinate importance, become the tests of Christian progress. It thus became common to exclude from the communion persons known to have danced, or to have played at cards [1]. The great object, lastly, of the early school, the promotion of practical, living Christianity around them, became a mere external duty, and being consequently pursued mechanically, alienated, too often, instead of winning to the Gospel.

It has been necessary to go through this painful detail, both as it is fruitful in admonition to our own, to all, times, and in that without it, the want of resistance from the school of the Pietists to the subsequent invasion of unbelief would be unaccounted for. It is obvious, however, that these observations relate to the diminution of its influence in its original seat, not to the branches, which in its earlier state it had sent forth. These may have been, and doubtless were, permanently as well as extensively influential, though the result of their insulated exertions

---

[1] Among other cases a Graf von Reuss (born 1717.) issued an edict to this purport. Mutual opposition seems to have occasioned the opposite excesses of the two parties; on this ground alone can be explained the blasphemous measure of an orthodox preacher, who published a formula of prayer to win at cards.

cannot be presented by history [1]. It is the misfortune of the history of all religion, that the silent but by far the largest influences which it exerts, those of individual and private life, can form no portion of the annals of mankind. An unfair, a very inadequate, too frequently an unfavorable, representation can alone result from the exclusive contemplation of the great phenomena, which public history records; the cases, in which religion has been made by bad men the instrument and the plea of ambition, the Inquisition, the devastation of America, the dragonnades of France, the expatriation of hundreds of thousands from that land, can be, and have been, faithfully recorded; of the blessings which it has produced not the thousand thousandth part is known to any but to Him, to whom alone all hearts are open; who has seen the evil and undisclosed passions, which it has, in silence, overcome; the sorrows it has cheered; the difficult duties it has given strength to perform; the kindly and benevolent feelings which it has produced; the hearts, in which the love of God has created, expanded, hallowed the love to man. A few such cases, a few of its great results, we are allowed to see, to weigh down the record of incidental evil; the immeasurably greater proportion is reserved for that day, in which all secret good, as well as secret evil, shall be discovered. Privacy is often the condition, as well as

[1] See Niemeyer, ibid. S. 56.

the natural element, of religious good. As the value of the great and fearful element, whose uses are so essential to us, is generally felt most in its privation; at other times, perhaps, we think chiefly of it, where it is most visible, in its destructive effects, in the devastations of the storm, or the conflagration of our cities, and forget, or cannot calculate, the innumerable hearths which it in silence cheers, the thousand comforts or necessaries of life, to which it is essential; so, and much more, is it with that spiritual fire, which first kindles into being the noblest energies of our nature, which, realizing, in a higher sense the heathen fable of man's formation, converts the sordid, inanimate, though well-formed, mass of clay, into a living spirit, warming and enlightening and purifying the best affections. By far the greater proportion of its influences can be known to none; and even of the slight proportion, which admits of being manifested in external action, most are witnessed but by few, in the narrow sphere of their immediate influence; collectively, none know them.

For the conduct of those, who, for worldly ends, in conscious hypocrisy, assumed the language, habits, and exterior of the Pietists, these are, of course, no farther responsible, than as, by adopting injudicious and insufficient tests, they may have facilitated the imposture. It afforded, however, large scope for misrepresentation and misconception. Opportunities for this deception occurred in Halle itself, and yet more in some of the courts of the lesser German princes[1]. At Halle, so soon as a particular tone or language came to be considered as indications of Christian piety, they were, of course, in many instances, adopted by students, who wished to obtain the offices at the disposal of the instructors. At some courts the use of the language, which had received the supposed stamp of piety, facilitated the advance, not only in ecclesiastical, but even in civil, offices. The hollowness thus occasioned was discovered at the death of these mistaken promoters of piety, when the tone of the court forthwith resumed its genuine and undissembled character[2].

It now remains only briefly to mention the scientific deflections to which the system was exposed. It is the natural and universal tendency of every school, on the one hand, to convert what was originally a predominant only, into an exclusive, character; on the other, gradually to lose sight of and to omit what at first occupied a subordinate, though essential, place. The aim of Spener, Francke, and the first Pietists was, we

---

[1] Among these were the courts of Graf Heinrich II. von Reuss; Graf von Stollberg-Wernigrode; Duke Ernest of Saalfeld; Prince August of Mecklenburg; and the King of Denmark. Great weight having been attached to the power of making long extempore prayer, as a sign of real conversion, a Duke of Coburg required the masters of schools to utter these in his presence, as a test of their fitness for advancement.

[2] This was especially visible at the courts of Wernigrode and Saalfeld.

have seen, to give theology a practical character; though they endeavoured to promote true science, still the practical results were their main object. The deflection, of course, was, in those who maintained the strict character of the school, that the practical character of Theology became all in all; that science was either lightly regarded or despised; in others, such as the in many respects valuable Baumgarten, the scientific element too largely predominated. The separation was the more natural, in that the two parts, the scientific and the religious interests, were rather united than blended in the first founders of the school.

Through these unhappy deflections, great as was the temporary influence of the first institution, permanent the benefits communicated in a narrower circle by individuals whom it had sent forth, and the indirect influence of its first teachers, when the irritation of party feeling was withdrawn, upon many who cannot be counted among its adherents, it was disabled, as a body, from opposing any effectual resistance to the inundation of unbelief, or from diminishing the rigidness of prejudice by which this re-action was in part produced. The rapid decay of this attempt to reform the barren orthodoxism by a recurrence to practical and unspeculating Christianity increased the apparent hopelessness of such a re-animation. The fanaticism coincident, and by the enemies of the effort identified, with it, alienated from the wish for a remedy. The rationalist tendencies of the age were promoted by this treble exhibition of the aberrations of belief, through which it was presented to the superficial or the presumptuous, as a speculative system, oppressive to the intellectual without communicating energy to the moral powers, as the garb of hypocrisy, or the dream of a bewildered imagination. Science was inlisted against it not only by its self-confidence in its own strength, but by the perversion in the orthodox, the contempt in the pseudo-pietist and fanatic, bodies, the opposition by all.

There was indeed one body of men [1], who,

---

[1] The chief characteristics of this class are clearness of views, good judgment, and well-digested learning, yet without either distinguished acuteness or depth of mind, or broad and general principles. As repertoria of information, their works are consequently valuable; they filled up some of the details of science, but were unable to advance its limits, or to give it a secure and large basis. The theological system might have received through their means a beneficial simplification, had a sufficient interval elapsed to permit it to be imperceptibly modified, but its character was too little pronounced to have much effect in the violent collisions which followed. Of the individuals mentioned Buddeus is duly appreciated among us, Mosheim is unfortunately principally known by a most unfaithful translation of one, and that not his best, work, from which a false estimate alone can be formed of his intellectual, moral, and religious character. The author has found, from collation, the original in so many cases offensively coloured and disguised by gratuitous interpolations of epithets, or of whole sentences, that collation seems to him absolutely indispensable, wherever it is of importance to know the precise sentiment or statement of Mosheim. A close translation would probably reduce the work to half its present size. Mosheim, besides his

though not belonging to the school of the pietists, would never have existed without their collision with the opposed system, such as Buddeus, Mosheim, Pfaff, &c. men of great learning, and practical minds, who acted beneficially in a limited sphere, and who would have been an ornament to any existing party, but who did not possess sufficient calibre or comprehensiveness themselves to form one, to give a permanent direction to the character of the age, or to satisfy the whole intent of its scientific requisitions. Their existence is however to be accounted among the benefits conferred by pietism, and they form a memorable historical phenomenon in the course of the new theological developement. More directly emanating from the Pietists was the school, which, descending from Bengel and Storr, remained amid increasing degeneracy, as witnesses of the practicability of the union of a deep piety, genuine orthodoxy, and scientific investigation; and who while they candidly admitted into their system the real advances of theological science, in part

works on Ecclesiastical History, which first raised the science in Germany above the character of a chronicle, and furnished an impartial estimate of the character of the opposed parties, was the author of several commentaries on Scripture, which, without great depth, were valuable for a good developement of the connection in each book. His work on Scriptural Moral, though not sufficiently scientific, has much that is valuable; his sermons long remained models of pulpit eloquence. (Schr. 41. 168. 43. 169. fg.) Pfaff commenced a reform in the mode of treating the types of the Old Testament, in Doctrinal Theology, and in the principles of Ecclesiastical Law.

successfully opposed the illegitimate innovations incidental to its earlier stages. Though some intellectual deficiencies limited their immediate influence, they were to a certain degree the patterns, as well as the precursors of what a maturer age is now richly completing. In their own times, even their moderate corrections of the faults of the received system were regarded with suspicion and refutations [1].

Before passing to the last systematic struggle, which the orthodox school had to encounter previous to the final conflict, two men of very different character, but both in some measure connected with the Pietists, may be mentioned, each of whom effected some alteration, if not in the system itself, yet upon the opinions of the times; Arnold and Thomasius. It affords, indeed, in itself, no small presumption of the untenableness of that system, that no attack was made upon it, (even previously to the altered character of those days, which witnessed its dissolution,) without producing some corresponding impression. Arnold originally belonged to the Pietists. A gloomy mind, and a want of sufficient confidence in Him, to whom all is possible, made him resign his Professorship at Giessen, from despair of producing any amendment in the dissolute habits of the students, yet unable, as he expresses it himself, to endure to see hundreds, who should hereafter have the cure of souls, but who never appeared

---

[1] See Semler Lebensbeschreibung, 2 Th. S. 146.

yet to have had a thought of their own. He afterwards applied his vast learning and ingenuity to the reform of ecclesiastical history; yet, misled by his dislike of the orthodoxism of his own days, and of the fruitless and wanton multiplication of heresies, as well as of the injustice uniformly perpetuated towards any whom the prevailing Church had on any occasion stamped as heretics, he manifested scarcely less partiality to all who had been so denominated, than had hitherto existed against them. There was, however, enough of truth in his views to shake the previously prevailing opinion, that the party, which succeeded for the time in establishing their own orthodoxy, was always in the right. The influence of Thomasius, (as, indeed, the general character of his mind was more calculated to destroy than to build up,) was rather exerted in the demolition of detached prejudices, and in the promotion of a greater freedom and independence of thought, than in producing any comprehensive innovation in the system. The bitterness, vehemence, and occasional buffoonery of his satire, was deservedly a further obstacle to his success. He removed, however, many insulated errors [1],

[1] Such were the importance of church ceremonies not ordained by Christ or the Apostles, (in his " Rechte Evangelischen Fürsten in Mitteldingen oder Kirchencärimonien"), the right of civil interference in matters of faith, except as far as concerns the public peace, (Das Recht Evangelischen Fürsten in Religionsstreitigkeiten,) the opinion that heresy implied perverseness of will, or was penal, (ob Ketzerei ein strafbares Verbrechen sey, and

I

and by the overthrow of the dominion of the Aristotelic philosophy prepared the way for the dominion of that of Wolf.

The previous conflicts had acted rather in diminishing the extent than in changing the character of the orthodox school, in detaching some portion of its empire, than in any change of its own internal constitution. The Wolfian philosophy was received into the system itself, and with the temporary appearance of adding to its strength, contributed, ultimately, to its fall. It seems, indeed, to have been the fate of every successive philosophy in Germany, to be at first indiscriminately opposed by the Theologians, and then to have been unduly admitted into their own science. Experience, and a surer ground of faith has now shewn them the right place of philosophy, as an auxiliary science, and subdued the hostility with-

---

" vom Rechte Evangelischen Fürsten gegen d. Ketzerei,") and many other points derived from, or connected with, these. He laid the foundation for the removal of numerous others by the study of ecclesiastical history, both for itself, (cp. Niemeyer, Univ. Halle, S. 47,) and as necessary for the understanding of ecclesiastical law; (Höchstnöthige Cautelen, welche ein studiosus Juris, der sich zur Erlernung der Kirchenrechts-gelahrtheit vorbereiten will, zu beobachten hat.) Schröckh, 42. 542. 548. He was opposed at the time by the theologians, especially by the oft-named Ben. Carpzov, but his services have since been acknowledged with gratitude, and himself styled the reformer of ecclesiastical law, (Schröckh, ib. Henke, iv. S. 252. 537. fg. 577, fgg.) It may be added, that he first removed in Germany the heathenish superstition of witches, sorcery, &c. so frequent a source of cruelty, the denial of whose truth B. Carpzov had declared a punishable offence. (Henke, ib. p. 581. fg.)

out producing the yet more unnatural identification[1]. The principal opposition, with which Wolf at first met, was from the Pietists, among whom he taught at Halle. The great importance, which he ascribed to the employment of his science in Theology, appeared to be dangerous; his adoption of Leibnitz's "predetermined harmony" to involve the admission of fatalism; his

[1] There are at present but few representatives of this system, such as Daub and Marheinecke, who have converted doctrinal theology into the philosophy of Schelling and of Hagel, and De Wette, who is too much influenced by that of Fries. As Bretschneider has placed Schleiermacher in this class, and the charge has been introduced into this country, it is but justice to that great man who, whatever be the errors of his system, has done more than (some very few perhaps excepted) any other, to the restoration of religious belief in Germany, to oppose to this assertion that of his distinguished and independent disciple, Twesten. (Ib. S. 199.) "Is it apprehended that the Nature-philosophy, amid its pretensions to absolute knowledge, will not respect the independence of the religious conviction, and only admit Christianity as far as it can introduce into it its own positions, or interpret it as a symbolical representation of them? through Schleiermacher has the peculiar and independent source of religion in the human mind, and *the original difference of philosophy and doctrinal theology* been set in so clear a light, that the invasion of the province of either by the other seems thereby to be adequately guarded against." It were contrary also to a maxim laid down by Schleiermacher himself. "The endeavour to introduce philosophical systems into theology is generally at variance with a correct interpretation of Scripture." Kurze Darstellung des theologischen Studiums, p. 51, a work, which, with a few great defects, is full of important principles and comprehensive views, and which will form a new era in theology whenever the principles which it furnishes for the cultivation of the several theological sciences shall be acted upon.

rejection of some former methods of proving the existence of a Deity, to lead to atheism. Though he was, however, himself banished, through the combined representations of the Theologians of Halle and of some individuals at Berlin, his system, through its clearness, definiteness, systematic spirit, and consistency, which satisfied the philosophical wants of the times, gained ground continually, and was further cultivated and developed by the adherents whom it acquired. Through these it maintained its ascendancy until near the 18th century. Within a few years after the banishment of Wolf, the first attempt was made by a theologian (Canz [1] of Tubingen) to in-

---

[1] In his Usus Philosophiæ Leibnitianæ et Wolfianæ in Theologia. 1728. The theological faculty of Tübingen destroyed all the copies of the third part of this work, which they could find. Canz was followed by Reinbeck, who had great influence in all matters of religion in Prussia under both Frederics; (he wrote " philosophic considerations upon the Augsburg Confession," which were continued by Canz and Alwahrdt;) by Ribov, Professor at Helmstadt and Göttingen, author of the " Institutiones Theologiæ dogmaticæ methodo demonstrativa traditæ," in which however he confines himself to the doctrines common to natural with revealed religion; by Schubert at Helmstadt and Greifswald; Carpov at Weimar; Darjes at Jena, who applied the Wolfian mode of proof without limitation to revealed doctrine, and neglected Scriptural evidence. Thus the eternity of future punishment was to be demonstrated by Schubert: Darjes thought to establish the doctrine of the Trinity by algebraical formulæ, (Tractatus philosophicus, in quo pluralitas personarum in Deitate, qua omnes conditiones, ex solis rationis principiis methodo mathematica demonstratur. 1735.) while Carpov applied the method in all its strictness to the whole existing system; suffice that the

troduce his system into Doctrinal Theology; others quickly succeeded; and these established in different parts of Germany, at Göttingen, Helmstadt, Berlin, Greifswald, Weimar, Jena, &c. formed different centres, whence it extended its influence by their oral instruction as well as by their writings. Notwithstanding the unquestioned Christian principles of its author, its reception tended to bring on the destruction of more

Trinity, *the nature and origin of the soul of Christ*, his conception, the imputation of Adam's sin, the incarnation of the Son of God, and the redemption of mankind thereby effected, the state of his soul after death, &c. were hence to derive their proof. ("Œconomia Salutis N. T. methodo scientifica adornata," in four 4tos.) This last, though opposed, was defended by very many; while none saw the extent of the evils of the system. (Schröckh, 43, S. 28—37. Schlegel, K. G. vi. 102—108. Henke, vii. 55.) The "Tentamen Theol. dogm. methodo scientifica pertractatæ" (1741. three 8vos.) of Wyttenbach, though a Swiss divine, had much influence, and was even used as a compendium for lectures in Germany. (Schlegel, S. 108, 109.) The evils of this system, as summed up even in the Allgemeine Deutsche Bibliothek, B. 2. S. 183, were, the introduction of philosophical positions into the system of religion; the equalizing what was certain or probable, problematical or established, what was left obscure in Scripture with what was clear; the neglect or arbitrary application of Scripture interpretation, the philosophizing with, not always out of the Scripture; "so that had this method been continued, Scripture had no longer been the *source* of religious knowledge, but at most, a witness only, which was to confirm by its evidence the conclusion which was already arrived at." Crusius, though in part opposed to this system, did not improve it; Scriptural proof occupied an equally subordinate place; the mode alone of philosophizing was changed. (Schröckh, ib. S. 41.) The author, however, survived his system.

than the system which it was called in to support, and to the encouragement of Rationalist principles. The faulty portions, indeed, of the previous system alone, would directly suffer from the spirit of deeper and more accurate investigation nurtured by this philosophy; yet indirectly it promoted many habits of mind, in part already existing, through which Christianity itself could not but be affected or mistaken. The disposition to give to reason not a negative merely, but a positive, decision in matters of faith was fostered by the habit of proving revealed doctrine by algebraical formulæ, or by philosophical grounds; the abstract mode of treating its subjects aggravated the evils of the existing system, already too exclusively speculative; uncertain philosophical tenets and hypotheses were introduced into the system of doctrine, as if equally established with Scriptural truth; the requisitions, which Christian evidence can be called upon to satisfy, were obscured by the confusion of mathematical and moral proofs; a large portion of that evidence lost by the exclusive appeal to the intellect; and finally, the already diminished consciousness of the positive doctrines of Christianity was yet further weakened by the fabric of natural Theology, formed by this system through the mere omission of what, in the prevailing religious ideas, was peculiarly Christian, and the substitution of proofs from reason for those from Scripture[1]; a skeleton, deprived of the form, and

[1] Twesten, S. 185.

beauty, and life of the once animated being. The ground-work of a bare deism, or naturalism, was thus already laid.

To sum up briefly then the internal state of things in Theology, at the moment when the struggle with the united and condensed efforts of unbelief of every age and of every country was about to commence, we find the result to be, an abstract and unpractical system, in which error was mingled with truth, yet these so blended together, that the practicability of a separation was scarcely seen either by the supporters or by the opponents, and the untenable human additions, advanced more prominently and defended as equally essential with the divine basis: we find the truths themselves presented in a dry dialectic form, destructive of their life and influence, and no distinction made between the rejection of the received mode of stating and explaining them, and the abandonment of the doctrines thus stated; none between those which are essential to Christianity, and those which, though forming part of its system, would if rejected, disfigure, but not destroy it: and, (which was the foundation of those perversions,) the maintenance of the letter of the whole system, as a sum of credenda, viewed as in itself *the* object of Revelation, without reference to the practical religious value; the efforts to make them practical regarded as hypocrisy or fanaticism, and the school, who had begun the undertaking, degenerate; the real proofs of the truths themselves overwhelmed and choked by a multitude of others, of evident invalidity, yet regarded as altogether essential to the maintenance of those truths; true science and free inquiry abandoned and opposed; Scripture scarcely felt to be the basis of religious truth, nor studied in order to discover it, and the right understanding of Scripture itself perplexed by wrong principles and obscured by the neglect of history; the knowledge of the nature, objects, and influence of Christianity, lost through the want of that best comment upon it, a Christian life, and the defect not even objectively supplied by the study of its past existence.

To this condition of Theology, must be added the moral and intellectual circumstances of the age: its moral character was such as might be anticipated from neglected education, and the defects in Christian teaching and Christian ministry,—frivolity, self-gratification, and corrupted morals [1]; nor was its intellectual character, though more difficult to condense, from the variety of the elements of which it was composed, less adverse to the subsistence of Christianity. It is indeed rare, either in individuals or nationally, that a state of strong excitement is not accompanied by a diminution of religious feeling; the absorbing gratification of active mental creation jars the tone of mind essential to the Christian influences; a feeling of self-confidence and self-satisfaction is generated, unfavourable at least to that deep sense of man's

---

[1] Schlegel, v. 246.

dependence, his insufficiency, and his necessities, which draws him to his God, and his Redeemer. Not the pursuit of science in itself, not the depth of speculation, but the engrossing power which they exert over the unaccustomed mind, (and to such an one only are they thus unhealthy,) interferes with the harmonious and proportionate developement of the intellectual and religious faculties. In the present instance, the impulse appears originally to have been given by the Leibnitz-Wolfian philosophy: this, without great speculative depth, imparted new energy to the German mind, as being the first effort to produce a self-originated and native system of philosophy; the eminent distinctness, precision, and force, which it in part discovered, in part communicated to, the German language, both rendered that language a fitter instrument for other exertion, and enabled it, (as language always does,) itself to re-act upon the activity of the mind: the study of history was revived and reformed through the views of Thomasius, and the acquaintance with our own literature: a number of highly-gifted minds were roused in every department, and German literature, in many branches at least, sprung with unexampled rapidity from infancy to maturity. Had a religious spirit been already there, this revival might have contributed, like the first and great re-awakening of literature in Europe, to the vindication and purification of the Evangelical belief; in the actual event, it furnishes an additional proof, that however reanimated science aided in, it was not a principal source of the Reformation. Like the shower, it may aid the seed to vegetate, but the seed it is not; the ground being now unprepared, it gave luxuriance to the natural productions, which choked it. The incidental causes which made a suddenly revived, and therefore as yet unsound, study of history especially injurious have been already hinted. It was the unsound part of the Wolfian philosophy also which was injurious.

These intellectual defects were again strengthened by the moral faults of the age. The conceit and absence of moral earnestness, then extensively prevalent, greatly promoted the natural liability of times of newly kindled energy to over-rate all supposed discoveries, and to depreciate indiscriminately every thing which before existed; to prefer extent to depth of investigation, and to be dazzled consequently by every specious novelty. For a time, at least, every hypothesis opposed to the strictness of the previous system, was assured, among a certain class, of a favourable reception; and though this disposition had ultimately the collateral advantage, that the truth was more clearly ascertained, through the examination of every imaginable opposed theory, as well as through the modifications which itself occasionally obtained from the persevering sifting of views, at first unpromising, the first result was the introduction into theology of much that was shallow and capricious. The evils however, which occurred must not be entirely ascribed to a prevailing love of innovation, being in part attributable to the contrary error of the previous and contemporary orthodox school, which refused altogether to listen to any theory at variance with its own, or the results of whose enquiries was a priori certain.

The collision, however, to which the German Theology must, it appeared, be necessarily exposed, might perhaps have been still deferred; the regeneration, by which it was to be restored, have been effected without this great struggle, but for circumstances connected with the reign of Frederic the Second. The extreme popularity given by the authority of that monarch to French literature, at that time universally tinged with a flippant unbelief, even in works not professedly written in mockery of religion; the reception of French unbelievers at his court and as his companions, some of them (such as the wretched La Mettrie and Voltaire,) the most reckless and unprincipled; and the countenance given in an admiring nation by his own professed opinions, aided strongly to determine in this direction the existing frivolity. Frederic, when he saw the moral effects of the extended unbelief, in vain repented [1] that he had contributed to its propagation. The disposition thus engender-

[1] It has been related to the author by one likely to be accurately informed, that Frederic shortly before his death, in expressing his regret at the altered condition of his dominions in this respect, professed that he would gladly sacrifice his best battle, could they but be restored to the state in belief and in practice in which he had found them.

ed was fostered by translations of the writings of all the principal deists of our own land.

The attack upon Christianity had been carried on more systematically [1] in our own, than in any other, country; the necessity of a revelation, as well as the validity of the several evidences for its truth had been successively disputed by men, some of whom possessed no ordinary acuteness: the course, which had been here adopted, was eminently calculated, from the similarity of its general character and of its defects, to promote the direction which the German mind was taking; inasmuch as the greater part of the early English unbelievers had been carried into unbelief partly by the same intellectual defects, partly by similar unhappy circumstances in the Church itself. The sunken state of Christianity through the civil wars, and the controversies of embittered

---

[1] There is scarcely a point in the whole compass of Christianity or of Christian evidence which was not, in a regular progression, sifted by the English Deists. Herbert, by substituting a natural theology for revealed doctrine, and by assigning man's natural instinct as the source of his knowledge of truth, the universality of the reception of those truths as the test of their being thus derived, laid a broad foundation for all the theories and criticisms of his successors. The distinctive character of the Christian miracles had been disguised by Blount; the morality of the Gospel criticised from a false point of view by Shaftesbury; the evidence from miracles and prophecy had been separately, (and therefore, as evidences, unfairly) judged by Woolston and Collins; the theory of rationalism had been proposed with plausibleness, consistency, and roundness, though without depth, by Tindal.

parties, induced in Lord Herbert of Cherbury, the leader of the English Deists, the attempt to remedy the unpracticalness of the existing system, by converting Christianity into a mere scheme of Ethics; they had led Toland to deny all higher truths of Revelation, and had inclined Hobbes to transform Christianity into a mere instrument of state policy. The similar consequences of the thirty years' war, in which, as in England, Religion was made the watchword, and to whose prolongation the contentions of religious parties had in part contributed, produced among many of the Germans a similar disposition. The constant appeal to the rationality of the system of Christianity which led Tindal to conceive of it as a mere "republication of the Religion of Nature[1]," was extensively encouraged in Germany by the translation of the works of the earlier English Apologists, and by the partly allied character of the orthodox school. The erroneous conceptions of inspiration and of prophecy, and the consequent failure to understand the connection of the two covenants, together with the exclusive ap-

---

[1] Tindal himself refers to a passage of Sherlock, in which this expression occurs, as well as the assertion that the laws of Christianity are a clear exposition of that original religion. Neither Bishop Conybeare nor Foster in their answers (which, however, are the most celebrated which appeared) pressed the necessity of the Christian revelation, but the former contented himself with shewing that it formed an useful addition to the religion of nature through its positive laws, the latter that its system of morality was superior to that naturally discovered.

peal to the intellect in the proposition of the evidences, which had confused to Collins the argument from prophecy, gave a ready access to his criticisms when transferred into the German Church. The depth of thought and of moral earnestness accordingly which guided Lord Herbert of Cherbury[1] in his search after the source of truth in the human mind, the acuteness of Toland[2] and of Hobbes, and the ability evinced in detached criticisms by Collins and Morgan[3], ex-

[1] Much moral as well as intellectual reflection is implied in the confession of Lord Herbert, that the understanding is an insufficient source of knowledge in divine things, as well as by his directing his mind to consciousness, (or as he called it instinct) as the only independent ground of such knowledge. The errors in the application of this truth he shared in common with Jacobi, with whom his general character has much similarity; yet notwithstanding these errors, he is entitled to a high degree of respect from the earnestness of his religious as well as from his intellectual character.

[2] It is remarkable in Toland that he was first carried on by the consecutiveness of his speculations to the only consistent system of unbelief, Pantheism. Locke says of him that but for his love of distinction he would have been a great man; and Leibnitz, whose annotationes subitaneæ ad Tolandi Librum (1707) are the best of the 50 refutations which appeared against him, praises his acuteness.

[3] Morgan put together with greater minuteness than any other the historical critical difficulties, and was much used both by the French and German unbelievers; (the most of Voltaire's objections, which do not originate in his own unprincipled inventions, are derived from Morgan and Tindal.) He manifested also no ordinary acuteness in the doctrinal objections which he adduced, while he won through his greater candour; from Collins whole sections have been transcribed into modern doctrinal works

erted greater influence, and that upon minds less frivolous or less morbid, than those acted upon by the wit and audacious falsehoods of Voltaire[1], or the diseased sensibility of Rousseau. Imitators, but for the most part with few original additions, were stimulated in Germany itself. Translations of our earlier English Apologists opposed to these works did but aggravate the evil, and increase the rationalist tendency[2]; partly because they had themselves been in some degree tacitly acted upon by the systems which they opposed, partly as being too exclusively intellectual, and lastly, because from the different stage in which German Theology then stood, their very defences contributed to expose some of its untenable, but

---

of Germany; his work obtained its credit from the previous misconceptions of prophecy, as a mere historical description of the future, and the confusion of prophecy and foretelling therein involved.

[1] As unbelief assumed a different character in each of the three nations according to the ruling turn of mind in each, so had each its separate class of readers: the French unbelievers, from the unsystematic character of their minds, and from their recklessness about the establishment of any fixed principles, followed individual objections into a minuter detail, but without reference to any general theory; they aimed at destroying, without attempting to replace, Christianity; the English Deists from the predominant practical character of our nation, were generally determined in their investigation by what appears to be of moral practical importance; the German, who, from his more speculative character, pursues enquiry for its own sake, followed his system with more consistency whithersoever it led him.

[2] This is especially remarked by Twesten, S. 189, 90. and is indeed the view of the most observing minds of Germany.

unyielded, points. It will appear scarcely credible to one unacquainted with those times, to what degree these agencies were furthered by a review established by Nicolai. Its object was to recommend every book opposed, not merely to Christianity, but to every earnest character of mind, while it passed over in silence, or held up to scorn, every work which favoured a belief in Revelation [1]. With little recommendation, except peculiarities of style, and the favourable disposition of its readers, its dicta were considered as oracles; and its party succeeded with no better means than their bold claims to the exclusive possession of 'sound reason,' and the audacity with which they accordingly decided upon Christianity, to drown any voice raised in opposition, to brand any antagonist as an intolerant enemy of illumination, if not as a Crypto-Catholic. This shallowness was promoted by the substitution of the rightly-called "Popular Philosophy," for that of Wolf, through such writers as Garve, Eberhardt, M. Mendelssohn, and Basedow. Incapable of deep or consistent speculation, they laid "sound common sense," (the usual refuge of shallowness, or of deficiency in speculative powers) as the basis of their philosophy, and of their criticisms of Christianity; a superficial empiricism was the ground-work of that mere shadow of Natural Religion, to which they reduced Christianity: and they themselves

---

[1] It commenced in 1768, and grew to 48 4to. Volumes.

scarcely suspected the precariousness of their own arbitrary structure, now that they had undermined the foundation of positive belief, and were consequently astonished at the Spinozism of Lessing, and at Jacobi's vindication of its consistency for the mere understanding. A shallow theory of Eudaimonism stood at the head of their system. " Happiness was the highest destination of man, the end to which it was the purpose of God to lead him; an intelligent pursuit of happiness its morality, and to find one's own happiness in that of others, the most elevated virtue, to which it rose [1]."

Theology, however, declined only gradually, by successive generations, and even at last but partially, into this school of unbelief. The form which itself latterly assumed, was not the cause but the result of this collision with unbelief, which its earlier stage had tended by reaction to produce. Not only did the first theologians, who incidentally, or by too exclusive or partial a following up of their systems, gave occasion to the superficializing or the rejection of Christian doctrine, Baumgarten, Ernesti, and Michaelis, themselves still firmly adhere to them, but some even

---

[1] Twesten S. 193, in whose words much of the immediately preceding statement of the external auxiliary causes of unbelief is conveyed; they do not rest, however, on his authority alone, but are in Germany universally regarded as occasionally contributing to unbelief; more, however, than the circumstances, which incidentally called into existence what was already formed, they cannot in their own nature be.

of their next disciples, as Semler and Morus, did not altogether abandon any fundamental article. The course, in which this declension was completed, was rather such as might have been expected from the previous mere intellectual conception of Christianity, the gradual deadening of the ideas peculiarly Christian, the unperceived substitution of mere moral doctrines, which bore more or less analogy to those of Christianity which were now longer understood, and finally the attempt to conciliate Rationalism by bringing down Christianity to its low and carnal standard, than that of direct and intentional opposition. The seed withered because it had no root in the heart. Each theologian attempted and strained to maintain as much of Christianity, as his own gradually altered tone of mind enabled him to understand; it was the natural and almost necessary consequence of a mere objective contemplation of Christianity, destitute of the insight afforded by personal experience, that the objects themselves should become gradually more and more faint and indistinct, until they at length faded from the sight, or were mingled, in the increasing dimness, with others to which, viewed from that distance, they bore more or less similarity. It has often been the case, not in nations merely but in individuals, where early Christian education has not been further developed by active religion, that Christian doctrines have first lost their freshness and vividness, and that finally, though habit has retained the same names, impaired religious perception has substituted far other and far lower meaning than that which they once possessed, when they were felt as well as acknowledged. If under ordinary circumstances they often continue apparently the same, the contact with unbelievers, or the mistaken attempt to recommend Christianity from a partial and compromising point of view, invariably discovers, as it often promotes, the half-conscious deviation.

Of the first Theologians who prepared for the new system, Baumgarten, who was a real Christian, though gradually chilled by the exclusive love of the mere scientific element of Theology, was chiefly influential by the introduction of English Theology of a freer, but very negative and superficial character; by the promotion of the study of history through the translation of English works; and by accustoming his disciples to depart from the traditional method, through the application of the form of the Wolfian system to the different branches of Theology. By this last innovation, especially, the Scriptural freshness, which Doctrinal Theology and Scriptural Interpretation had recovered in the school of the Pietists, was in that same school in a different mode destroyed. The tabular method, the dialectic precision, the abstract language, which he employed, humanized and straitened the divine truth; the fulness of the Christian ideas admits not of being compressed into narrow logical formulæ; the free and living spirit, which animated its language, evaporated in the minute dissection of this dialectic anatomy. Many of Baumgarten's disciples[1] were led by this method to a mere cold intellectual conception of Christianity; and Semler, whose naturally ardent mind was capable of deeper impressions, inherited from his teacher only the views of reform, which Baumgarten recommended as necessary[2], but felt himself too old to execute, and which Semler, from the inaccurate and unsystematic character of his mind, ill, because imperfectly and partially, developed. Equally faithful to the sum of Christian doctrine remained Ernesti, even in his later years, when it had already been pared down by theologians to a mere "republication of the Religion of Nature." In him, however, the evil effects of a mere external conception of Christianity were yet more apparent. His revival of the "grammatical," as opposed to the doctrinal, interpretation of Scripture, was indeed a great and very beneficial change; a change for which the

---

[1] Besides Semler, many of the principal innovators, as Büsching, Teller, Spalding, Eberhardt, Steinbart, &c. had been pupils of Baumgarten. (Niemeyer, d. Univ. Halle, S. 104.) The influence of Baumgarten was greater probably than that of any other individual; almost all the theological students of Halle, (never fewer than between 5 and 600, and often more,) attended his lectures; the attachment to the letter of his lectures was so great, that they were not only at the time transcribed by most of his pupils verbatim, but were published after his death with diplomatic accuracy, different MSS. being collated and even minute variantes noted, according to the several years of the delivery of the lectures. Even Baumgarten's bodily defects were imitated. (Niemeyer Ebend. S. 77, 81.)

[2] Semler Lebensbeschr. ap. Niemeyer, S. 104.

German Church must long be grateful to him, in that it has restored the principle of the Reformation, that not human system, but the clear word of God in the Scripture, is the basis and norm of faith. Too exclusively intent, however, on the introduction of the classical rules of interpretation, he slighted the historical element: and destitute of the key which would have opened to him the fuller riches of Scripture, he forgot that every new religion must form to itself a new language, that in order to convey new truths, words already in use must indeed be employed to connect them with the previous ideas of mankind, but that the signification of these words must be modified, that they must be re-cast, re-moulded, in order to receive the stamp of the newly communicated truth. The application of classical language in its full strictness to the records of Christianity, could but convert them into a document of mere human speculation. That λόγος signified " reason," and " wisdom" in the classics, was a very superficial, as well as an entirely mistaken, ground for supposing that in St. John it meant nothing more than the wisdom of the communication made to man.

The effect of this mistake is seen in its full perniciousness in his immediate followers [1]. " Regeneration" was supposed to signify " the mere reception into a religious society;" the doctrine

---

[1] E. g. Fischer (who was indeed no theologian, but did influence theology) Proluss. de Vitiis Lexicon N.T., Schleusner, &c.

of the influences of the Holy Spirit became, more or less, a certain attaining of praiseworthy qualities with the (often merely external) assistance of God; the ἓν εἶναι with the Father, an unity of disposition or of will.

A similar failing, arising from the same source, is manifest in Ernesti's mode of vindicating received doctrine. Thus in claiming inspiration for the books of the Old Testament, he even admits the supposition, that they may not be calculated for all mankind, that they did not tend to the improvement of the human heart. He acknowledged their temporary value for the Jews, but did not feel their direct importance for Christians[1]. In the school of experience of Luther, he would have learnt the analogy of different parts of the life of most Christians to the two different stages of the Law and the Gospel; he would have felt the necessity of the law, even now, as a state of preparatory discipline to bring us to Christ.

The adherence of Michaelis to the established system, and his respect for religion is probably mainly to be attributed to the impressions made by the intercourse of the Pietists, among whom he was educated by his father, the excellent J. H. Michaelis. Too light-minded, as himself says, to adopt their tone of pious feeling, he yet retained an external conviction of the truth of

---

[1] Neuester Theol. Bibliothek, B. 2. S. 440. fg. in his critique upon Semler's " Enquiries on the Canon of the Old Testament."

Christianity, endeavoured to remove objections by new theories, and much to the surprise of his younger contemporaries, held to the last many parts of the older system, which had been modified or laid aside. Throughout are the pernicious consequences of his mere outward persuasion manifest. Destitute of that conviction, which can alone give a comprehensive insight into the real character of Revelation, and the harmonious relation of its several parts, he had no guide which might enable him to perceive what might be safely admitted, without detriment to the system itself; he consequently, according to the usual error of persons taking only a partial view, frequently opposed the objection, instead of the principle, upon which the objection was founded; endeavoured to remove it by theories in conformity with mere human systems, and strengthened it equally by his concessions, and by his own inadequate and arbitrary defences [1].

[1] There is no work probably of Michaelis, at all touching upon religious subjects, to which these observations do not apply; "the Commentaries on the Laws of Moses," and "the Notes on the Old Testament," are full of these perverted applications of mere civil, often of modern, principles, unfounded theories and low views; his translation of the Bible indicates his common-place conceptions of Scripture: his "History of the Resurrection" evidences occasionally both his wrong principles of defence, and a readiness, which he seems to have deemed praiseworthy, to abandon his previous belief, in case it should be found to be false; his commentary on "the three most important Psalms concerning Christ" is a specimen of his failure, from want of enlarged views, to see the right principles of exposition, and the arbitrary

To a mind possessed of no enlarged principles, every minute difficulty obtained an intrinsic and perplexing force; his belief was a reed, ready to be shaken by every fresh breeze; all which had been previously won, seemed again staked upon the issue of each petty skirmish, and in the very descriptive comparison of Lessing on this sort of combatants, he was like the timid soldier who loses his life before an outpost, without once seeing the country of which he would gain possession[1]. The

theories and unsound criticisms to which he was consequently driven, &c. Deep insight into religion were indeed inconsistent with the intemperate habits and low moral character of Michaelis, which defiled his books occasionally, and still more frequently his lectures, with obscenity. It is a very characteristic trait of Michaelis's mind, that he himself records his having asked his father on his death-bed, which of the Lexica of Castelli he thought the best. (Pref. to Mich. Syr. Chrestomathie.) One may very consistently acknowledge the service, which Michaelis, and even Paulus, has rendered, by contributing to place the historical circumstances of Scriptural narration more before our eyes, to put us more in the situation of contemporaries, and to render the mode of conception less abstract, and yet esteem the manner in which they have done it pernicious, and derogatory to Scripture.

[1] Such, according to Lessing, was the conduct of theologians; the Christian he compares with the bold conqueror who, neglecting the fortresses on the frontier, at once takes possession of the land. "Never," he says, "will any one arrive at a belief in the Christian Revelation who thinks he must first clear up this or that doctrinal or historical minutia, before he accepts the substance; rather will he only ever accept all the several historical truths, who has first gained possession of the inward holy truth, and not the details." In this he was preceded by our great Bacon, who compares such defenders or enquirers to one, who, in order to light up

disadvantages, however, to which he thus exposed the defence of Christianity, were the least evils of the system; far more resulted from the common-place views of the persons, actions, institutions, and doctrines of Scripture, to which it gave rise: not only the theories of Eichhorn, (his pupil)[1] constructed on the assumed human origin of every phænomenon in revealed religion, but even the low and vulgar tone of mind, in which Paulus degraded every thing spiritual and divine in the Gospels to the sphere of civil every-day life, the mean and earthly principles which he attributes to its actors, (by which far more injury has been produced than by the soon exploded and now almost forgotten explanations of the miracles,) seem but the natural and inevitable consequence of this exclusion of religion from the theories of Michaelis.

Theology, thus already on the decline, naturally sunk still further, though in very different degrees, in the next generation; in Semler, the pupil of Baumgarten and of Ernesti; in Morus, the inheritor of Ernesti's principles; and in

a large hall, were to place a light in every corner, instead of one great central light, which should illumine every the most distant part.

[1] The pursuit of novelty, to the comparative disregard of truth, which was the besetting temptation of this original and elegant, but ill-regulated mind, revenged itself upon him; more fertile in new theories than any of his contemporaries, he survived to see the last extorted from him. His errors, however, must not be set to the account of German Theology, since he was a philosophical, not a theological, Professor.

Eichhorn and Koppe, the disciples of Michaelis. Of these Morus and Koppe superficialized still further the Christian ideas; Morus especially, devoid of any settled principles, though in his Epitome of Christian Doctrine he opposed none of the Christian doctrines, led the way to their subsequent rejection, by his representations of the uncertainty of the conflicting views; yet more perhaps by the arbitrary principle, which this hesitation caused him to propose in his doctrinal lectures, that so much only should be retained as tended to moral improvement. What was described to be thus uncertain, his disciples, naturally very inadequate judges of what was really practical, of course laid aside.

Not only however was there in these men no direct opposition, but the influence even of Semler, the most direct founder of the innovating school, lay more in the principles which he introduced, and in his own intellectual defects, than in any direct rejection of fundamental doctrines. The piety of his early days accompanied him in some measure through life, and became in his later years still more decided. His intellectual character was a singular combination of great advantages and great defects. On the one hand he possessed amazing retentiveness of memory, and very considerable acuteness: on the other he was entirely devoid of all philosophical talent, all power of extensive survey, of clear perception, and of accurate reasoning. His extensive reading supplied consequently only a mass of facts and ideas, which floated indistinctly before him; his acuteness suggested continually a number of minuter combinations, which his mind was not sufficiently systematic to correct or limit by reference to the whole subject to which they related, or to perceive the consequences to which they led. When in his latter days he saw how his principles had been developed by others, he repented that he had gone so far[1]. Against the Wolfenbüttel Fragments he wrote with earnestness; he opposed conscientiously, and prevented the appointment of Bahrdt as Professor at Halle: he preserved himself (however difficult the mode may be to understand) from the results of his own scientific investigation, by what he called his " private religion," (the religion apparently of feeling, whose separate and independent validity he wished to establish); and some of his theories, which have been most extensively abused, seem to have owed their character to the indefiniteness and obscurity with which he conveyed them. In his treatises on dæmoniac possessions[2] there was nothing in any wise dero-

[1] Niemeyer, Semler's letzte Äusserungen über religiöse Gegenstände, S. 9. He thought, however, that in an age which had been more adapted to the reception of these views, they could have been developed without injury.

[2] Semler came upon this subject not in the way of mere speculation, but to remove an injurious superstition, through which an hysterical person had been treated by a clergyman of high office near Wittenberg as actually possessed. Semler's first treatise went no further than to disprove present possessions, admitting the moral influence of evil spirits; his subsequent essay proposed only to prove that $δαιμονιζόμενοι$ need not, any more than

gatory to the Evangelists, much less any thing implying any 'accommodation' in Christ; yet his undistinguishing contemporaries pronounced the opinion to be irreconcileable with faith and piety, or proceeded[1] to deny the existence of any agent of evil superior to man. The indiscriminate stiffness of the preceding age yet survived sufficiently to perpetuate the reaction which it had caused; and a shallow generation, accustomed by the still continued mode of handling the subjects of Theology, to regard them as mere theoretical problems, seems to have thought, that the only mode of recovering liberty was to depart as widely as possible from the system which had fettered them. Every hint was eagerly seized, and under the protection of a certain correspondence with the views of those whose only aim was to attain that freedom of enquiry[2], which is an essential principle of

---

δαιμονᾶν, &c, in classic Greek, signify more than a "raging phrenzy," while he allowed that some narrations implied a stronger external or internal agency of the evil principle. Yet these treatises produced such works as the " Disquisitio an Adæmonismus cum *fide et pietate* Christiana conciliari possit." Tüb. 1763. The subject occupied subsequently, very unprofitably and unpractically, but to a wide extent, the German pulpit.

[1] E. g. Teller's Wörterbuch.

[2] A good view of the previous stiffness of the German Theology may be collected from the second part of Semler's Autobiography, in which he describes the progress of the developement of his own views, S. 121. fgg. We find then, in the province of Biblical Criticism, not only the letter, but the very variantes, (Kri, Chethibh,) of the text of the Old Testament supposed to be inspired, and this immutability of the text to be indispensable to

Protestantism, others found admission, who differed from them in their first principles, as well

the truth of Christianity; bolder critics, as Simonis and Le Clerc, accounted among evil-intentioned antiscripturarii; (S. 121-3.) the divine origin of the Hebrew points and accents maintained; the possibility of errors of transcription rejected; the Hebrew text considered as the norm of all versions, (S. 123.) yet the fable of Aristeas still retained; (S. 128.) the imaginary pre-eminent sanctity of the Hebrew language, and other inventions of the Rabbins, inherited; any innovation regarded as a petulant opposition to the agreement of the universal Church. (S. 130-2.) Every merely historical book of the Old Testament, as Ruth and Esther was further considered equally indispensable and essential to the beneficial reception of Christianity with those of the New Testament, and the discovery of Christ in all the books of the Old Testament to be a truth essential to religion, the basis of all interpretation, and the criterion of its soundness. (S. 135—144.) The perfect purity of the Greek of the New Testament was vindicated; (S. 126.) the relative value of its documents, which Luther, as well as the early Church, had acknowledged, was obliterated, and inspiration regarded as a mere mechanical act. (S. 161.) In Ecclesiastical History, the principles on which it had been cultivated in the Romish Church were still perpetuated; there prevailed an indiscriminate panegyric of the early orthodox, a severe condemnation of all the heretics of the first five centuries, without an historical acquaintance with either; it was yet full of exaggerated accounts of the early persecutions and martyrs: and (here equally as in the case of Gibbon) the indiscriminate admission of the later miraculous legends, and among these even of the least credible class, those by which the orthodoxy of one of conflicting speculations was to be established, endangered the reception of the miracles of the first introduction of Christianity. The whole study was confined for the most part to what related to the external society. (S. 154—161.) Symbolical, as well as doctrinal, theology, needed also extensive simplification, though the limits of a note will not allow even a condensed exhibition of this portion of the subject.

as in their object, but were included in the same category by the adherents of the traditional scheme. Science, unnaturally separated from Theology, whose end should be a scientific statement of divine truth, became its foe. It was from this cause alone, that the revival of historical interpretation by Semler became the most extensive instrument of the degradation of Christianity. The principle, that an historical religion cannot be understood without the history of the era of its introduction, that no writing can be fully understood without a knowledge of other contemporary writings, which fully develope the ideas, to which itself occasionally alludes, which it modifies or corrects, nor without a clear view, whether collected from itself or from exterior sources, of the persons with reference to whom it was originally written, and the circumstances which immediately occasions it, is so obviously correct, that in this country, where the circle of expounding Scripture by the system which has been founded upon it, has never been systematically adopted, the contest about the "Historical Interpretation" must be matter of surprise, and, until explained by previous circumstances, of perplexity. The principle had already in part been developed by Baumgarten: the unsystematic and unclear mind of his disciple saw neither the limits, by which it must in its own nature be circumscribed, nor the other principles by which it must be conditioned. The fundamental errors of Semler's application of it are the same which have already been noticed in

Ernesti; the same exclusive adherence to his single principle, the same failure to perceive the connection [1] of the Christian with the Jewish revelation, as the completion of this earlier education of mankind, the same inability to discriminate between what was principally intended for contemporaries, and what is directly also of eternal value; they were derived in part from the same source, the want of that deeper insight into the nature of the religion, which a constantly improving personal Christianity alone can give. Such

---

[1] This connection of the two dispensations had been in great measure obliterated by the Orthodox system, partly from overlooking the gradual character of Revelation, and finding every thing already fully revealed under the preparatory covenant, partly from the neglect of the historical interpretation: the study of the Apocryphal books, or of Philo, which supply a necessary link in the chain, by shewing how revealed truth had, during the temporary cessation of any new discoveries, been developed by human reflection in conformity to the earlier Scriptures, had been altogether neglected; the revelation in the New Testament had consequently become insulated and abstract; and Semler's principle, that " Revelation must consist of purely unknown truths," " that it was unworthy of it to say anew what had been already said," was a natural consequence of this system. It was this dogma, however, which most injured Semler's great principle of historical interpretation. It followed from this that Revelation could not be merely confirmatory, that whatever in it did agree with what previously existed, was mere $\xi v \gamma \kappa a \tau \acute{a} \beta a \sigma \iota \varsigma$; that whatever had been previously taught by the Pharisees, (though in fact indirectly derived from the earlier revelation,) could form no part of the later communication. On the same principles, however, even the meagre portion, yet left, of that scheme of truth, which was destined to regenerate mankind, must be still further reduced.

inexperience alone could convert the everlasting contrast of σάρξ and πνεῦμα into the mere temporary contrast of the Judaizing and narrowing conception of Christianity, with the freer views which St. Paul taught; have divided consequently the books of the New Testament into those in which the σάρξ, and those in which the πνεῦμα, predominated, or have conceived that the *sole* object of the Epistle to the Romans, was to oppose the particularism of the Jews, and to prove that the heathen also might attain eternal life. The theory of accommodation was an unavoidable consequence of this perverted form of historical interpretation. Still more injurious would the same system obviously be to the right understanding of the Old Testament, while the inducement to apply it was increased, by the inability of Semler to comprehend an extensive scheme, and by the greater faultiness of the system, which he could not but oppose. The confusion, further, which the orthodox system of Doctrinal Theology had introduced between essentials and non-essentials, biblical truth, and human developement or mode of statement, and the want in Semler himself of the deep Christian knowledge, and clearness of thought, which would have enabled him to unravel it, rendered his vast study of Christian doctrine in its earlier forms an inextricable labyrinth, a mere source of perplexity and uncertainty. The mind, long accustomed to derive its Christian knowledge from the mechanical study of the letter of a confined form, had lost the clue, which would have enabled it to trace in this variety of statements, and in what, to a superficial mind, appeared to be contradictions, the unity of the same spirit manifesting itself in various forms, according to the character of the individuals through whom it was conveyed. The former school had found in the Bible itself all the subsequent developements, which later speculation on its truths had subsequently, often indeed rightly and consistently, evolved: a superficial age, dazzled with the suddenness of the discovery, that parts of the received system were by time alone thus developed, and convinced only of the untenableness of that system, employed itself in remarking and accumulating the apparent differences: the higher unity in which much of this discordance would have harmonized, lay beyond their sphere. Doctrinal Theology assumed consequently in this school a critical and negative, rather than a positive, character: the sum of doctrine, considered as certainly fixed, gradually diminished, the developement of the connection even of the general truths of Religion became less frequent, and in the energetic description of the often-quoted author, who has, with the deepest insight, and soundest judgment, traced the whole course of doctrinal Theology, " they cleared with great exertions the site of the overthrown palace from the encumbering heap of ruins; they dug deep trenches to bring better materials to light; but as if their strength were exhausted with these efforts, they left it to each individual to put together a petty hut for his own use, if he should find the foundations still safe, and the materials adequate to the purpose; or, if they undertook the trouble for him, it was but a temporary construction, which, in its turn, was again to be laid in heaps [1]." Against these principles and this conduct of Semler, (which, it must again be repeated, arose from no indisposition to the doctrines [2], but originated in his sense of the necessities of Theology, and were perverted only by the indistinctness of his views) little opposition seems to have been made, (at least none is recorded,) though they led to the ultimate temporalizing and annihilation of every thing peculiarly Christian in the system; while long-enduring contests were excited by his partial deviation from the received opinion on dæmoniacs, or from his doubts with regard to some few of the least important biblical books,

---

[1] Twesten's Dogmatik, S. 244.

[2] That part of Semler's autobiography, which relates to his views in doctrinal Theology, (2 Th. S. 220, fgg.) indicates great earnestness of mind, and a practical object; and leaves, in common with every other part of this interesting piece of self-observation, a very favourable impression of his piety and conscientiousness. A misinterpretation of the word 'liberalis,' in Semler's Apparatus ad *liberalem* N. T. interpretationem, has given rise to misconceptions of his character in several English authors, and especially the late valuable Conybeare; (Bampton Lectures.) Semler did not hereby mean that false spirit which casts aside, under pretence of liberality, what from its own altered character it no longer values, but he wished to characterize his own theory, founded solely on the results of historical investigation, and *free* and independent of the previously established doctrinal system.

with regard to which, in the early Church, free scope had been permitted to difference of opinion. The orthodox school guarded with vigilance the number of the repositories of their treasures, but were unable to detect the substitution by which these treasures were deprived of their value. It is also remarkable, (as far as may be inferred from the yet very imperfect and inadequate history of the times,) that the opponents of succeeding aberrations were, with a few splendid exceptions, principally the practical clergy. These, in whom their difficult practical duties perpetuated the sense that something more was necessary than doctrinal speculation or a religion of nature, and thus kept alive the spirit of piety awakened by Spener, remained doubtless, to a very wide extent, unaffected by the contagion around them.

Scriptural doctrine having thus been converted into speculation by one party, superficialized by another, and treated as uncertain and vague by a third, there remained but one more declension, to which, under the then circumstances, all these systems tended, the final amalgamation namely of Christianity with the more earnest of the systems by which it was opposed, but to which it had been gradually approaching. What was left of Christianity was too little substantial to present any obstacle to this now natural union; nor is there any reason to doubt the assertion of the author[1] of

---

[1] Steinbart Philosophische Unterhaltungen zur weitern Aufklärung der Glückseligkeitslehre Heft. 3. 1786.

this last measure, that his object was to lead the sceptics of his time to the acceptance of Christianity. One of the most pious of his opponents [1] regarded his enterprize as a sincere, though unhappy, attempt to conciliate such of his contemporaries as felt the necessity of religion, but either knew not, or doubted, pure Christianity. The character of Steinbart seems to have been determined partly by a too ascetic early education, partly by the habit of a mere intellectual and subtle consideration of Christian truth, which was engendered by the study of the over-refining method of Baumgarten [2]. The two elements of religious-scientific knowledge were in him never combined. The perusal of Voltaire, which at first produced pain and disquiet, gained a gradually increased influence over his exclusively intellectual conviction; and while his early education preserved in him a regard to virtue with a general reverence towards God, and the study of the apologetic works of Locke and Foster infused a respect towards Christ, the perception of the errors, which the reference to experience alone, as the sole source of Christian knowledge, had occasioned in his pietistic teachers, fostered in him the far more dangerous tendency altogether to neglect it. His system consequently, though sincere, was miserably shallow. As happiness in

---

[1] The excellent Lavater in Pfenninger's Christl. Magazin.
[2] See the account of Steinbart in Schlegel. B. 6. S. 523. fgg.

his view is the only object proposed to man, so are human passions the only impediment; and the sum of the benefits conferred through Christianity is, that it promotes that happiness by awakening the reflection of mankind to their real and common good, and by the removal of the idea of arbitrary requisitions on the part of God, which impede the right working of reason, and perplex the natural conscience; that it contains a perfect system of moral; strengthens through its authority the natural suggestions of reason by the knowledge of the superintendance of God, by the hope of future rewards, and by the employment of prayer; gives an insight into the predominance of present good, and an anticipation of unbounded progress in various perfection. All deeper views of the holiness of God, of the spiritual degeneracy and spiritual capabilities of man, and of the means by which the lost energy may be restored, every thing in Christianity peculiarly Christian, and even the more earnest aspirations of the natural man, are wanting: " The system of pure philosophy, or Christian doctrine of happiness[1]" was neither philosophy nor Christianity, but served, after having been much disputed, to reconcile them in the degraded state in which they then existed [2].

[1] See the abstract of the above-mentioned work, ap. Schlegel, S. 527, fgg.

[2] Lessing, as he was throughout opposed to the shallowness of the popular philosophy, speaks also strongly against this unnerving of Christianity, with a view to render it acceptable. " Formerly," says he, " a wall of partition was drawn between Theo-

The two most distinguished of his opponents, Seiler and Sixt, Steinbart maintains, differ only in words from himself[1].

The work was now completed; and until a more earnest spirit should re-awaken the susceptibility for, and the need of pure Christianity, the gradations of the several classes mattered but little; whether, as Nösselt and others, they deprived the doctrines of Christianity of their high and efficacious import, or Socinianized them with Teller and Spalding[2], or rationalized them with

logy and Philosophy, behind which each might hold on its own course. What is done now? They break the wall down; and, under the pretence of making us rational Christians, make us irrational philosophers." Lessing compares further the theologians of this class to the master of a house, who, while he reviles the thief, himself throws his goods out of window, so that he has only to fetch them.

[1] In his "Philosophische Unterhaltungen," Heft. 1, ap. Schlegel, S. 545.

[2] Both Teller and Spalding belonged to a secret institute, (of which Mendelssohn, Nicolai, and other adherents of the popular philosophy, were also members), whose object was to re-model religion, and alter the form of government. Both, however, saw the necessity of proceeding slowly, and wisely confined themselves to the unnerving Christianity, by substituting common-place moral notions for its energetic doctrines, declaring these to be of importance only to the Theologian, or polemizing against them under the title of the oriental idioms of the New Testament. Thus unnerved, it would collapse at once, or at least offer no resistance. Thus they exchanged the doctrine of the influences of the Holy Spirit for the moral endeavours after improvement with the *external* assistance of God: for "regeneration" was adopted "resolution to lead a new life;" for "sanctification," "moral improvement;" for being "actuated by the Holy Spirit," "to live

the followers of Steinbart: nor can that mode of dismissing the evidences of prophecy and miracles, which, without expressing any unbelief in them, considered them as valid only for former times, well be considered as any additional step. It was but casting away the shell when the seed of future fruit was already gone. Buttresses, massive as these, were needed to aid in the support of the important fabric, as it once had stood, but to what avail to leave them when this was shrivelled up and dissolved?

The object of this Essay, which is but to hint the probable efficient causes of the temporary reception of rationalism into German theology, and the points of its gradual declension, not to give a view of that theology generally, has necessarily produced an almost exclusive attention to the dark side of the picture. Yet it would be an unjust and untrue representation, if it were not distinctly stated, that this outline is intended to convey only the predominant character of the age, that many at all times were found, in whom the struggle of contending opinions produced already its ultimate destination,—that of separating evangelical truth from scholastic systems, and of

---

in conformity to reason." Spalding had most influence through his essay on the Utility of the Preacher's Office; Teller, through his Lexicon to the New Testament, of which six editions were circulated. These, however, were among the rarer instances of practical clergy, who actively engaged in the promotion of the new system, as they are among those of men, who were actuated by impure, not merely by shallow, views.

'grounding it upon a firmer basis; who, though they could not dispel the gathering darkness, still sent forth even beyond the comparatively narrow sphere, which they directly illumined, the beacon-light of truth, and were instrumental in transmitting the sacred torch to an age where it could shine more freely, and more unimpeded. It would be unfair moreover to omit the mention of such men as Klopstock and Claudius, who, though not theologians, exerted an extensively beneficial influence upon their own and succeeding times; Klopstock, yet more by the Christian piety of his Religious Odes, than by his far famed epic; Claudius, by a very rare and happy union of distinguished talents and rich imagination, a genuine, though not deeply speculative, philosophical spirit, with the purest simplicity of mind, and a depth of Christian feeling and piety, which communicated its own chastened holiness and practical character to every subject which it treated. "Out of the fullness of the heart the mouth spoke," and therefore spoke naturally and to the heart. This Christian piety shed throughout an unobtrusive light, which was often principally perceived in the richness, and life, and truth, which it gave to the objects more immediately prominent. Nor is the love, with which the works of this genuine German author have been ever since cherished by his nation, a slight proof of the Christian disposition existing.

It does not belong to a brief sketch to give a detailed account of all the individuals who were borne along by, and swelled the tide of innovation. None of these later followers contributed any original views; the torpid influences of the popular philosophy, the proud and self-complacent satisfaction in the triumph which they were gaining, the increasing efficacy of French literature in the extension of the reigning French frivolity, indisposed to any deeper inquiries, which might endanger their tranquil possession of the exclusive claim to " sound reason." A system which originated in the mere negation of what preceded, in a mere abstraction of its deeper thoughts, could not in itself produce any thing positive. This hollow composition between reason and belief stifled for a time the longings of nature, which a more consistent and uncompromising system never fails again to recall; the emptiest and most timid schemes of unbelief are ever the most dangerous to Christianity; they are palliatives, which while they deaden the mind, and cast over it a paralyzing torpor, conceal the extent of the disease, and suspend the deeply-implanted wish for its real removal. The first new energy was consequently given by one far more opposed to the popular philosophy than to an historical revelation. A minute account then of the innovating theologians would present only a series of modifications of the leading classes, differing in the degree in which they unnerved Christianity, or as to the portions of it, which they admitted into their religion of reason, but agreeing in their general principles; and the survey, though necessary in a history, which would represent the state of German Theology during this period, and appreciate the extent of the existing evils, would in the present case, where the object is merely to trace the outline of the general course, only serve to distract the mind by advertence to subordinate points. Still less is it necessary to mention the different critical investigations with regard to the authenticity of several of the books of Scripture: these furnish but rarely, or at most only incidentally, any indication of the dispositions of the enquirers. The faith of the Christian depends not upon the reception of the one or the other book of Scripture; and it has been a supposition pregnant with mischief, that any doubt respecting an individual portion of the sacred volume necessarily implies a diminished value for its whole contents, or a weakened reverence and gratitude towards its divine Giver. The enquiries in Germany, though occasionally carried on upon wrong principles, seem generally to have had truth for their object, have contributed to the firmer and better-grounded establishment of several books, and to the better classification of all; and one instance at least, the anxiety evinced by practical as well as scientific Theologians to vindicate to its author what all Christianity has designated as 'the evangelical, the spiritual Gospel,' implies no slight interest in the truths which it pre-eminently contains [1].

[1] Within a short time after Bretschneider's collection of objec-

Two men, however, must be mentioned, belonging to this age, to whom much attention must be given in any view of the course of the final developement of this crisis; who, (though the one seems to have remained embarrassed to the last by the perplexing conflict of the different systems in Theology and Philosophy, the other, though he defended Christianity, knew it not in its depth, and defended it consequently on wrong principles,) both contributed to its re-establishment, and both contain, at least in the germ, many of the ideas, whose subsequent expansion and scientific justification has led to a correcter conception, a readier admission, and a deeper foundation, of its truths:—Lessing and Herder. It is difficult to appreciate how far Lessing stood within Christianity: how far his high value for it went beyond an objective esteem for its contents: how far his conception of "its internal holy truth" enabled him to overcome his historical and doctrinal difficulties and his inclination to Pantheism, and to

tions or difficulties relating to the genuineness of St. John's Gospel appeared, no less than fourteen answers were published; and the point is now established to the satisfaction of Bretschneider himself, in common with the rest of Germany; it would, however, be very unjustifiable to ascribe to Bretschneider any other motive than that which he assigns in his original work, the wish to bring the question to an issue: where doubts have acquired a general prevalence, it is an unquestionable service to collect those doubts as strongly as they are capable of being put; the only result of the desultory answers with which, till this is done, vindicators often content themselves, is to produce an unjustified and unconvinced conviction.

appropriate it to himself independently of its historical basis. A too predominant indulgence of the taste for elegant literature and the arts, in which he was so great a master, seem to have enervated in him the moral earnestness, and precluded him from the self-knowledge, necessary for a thorough and satisfactory examination; and though he perhaps rightly preferred Pantheism to the then existing systems, he had neither boldness to take the " saltum mortalem," by which Jacobi escaped it, nor a philosophy sufficiently deep to see the deficiencies of Pantheism itself[1]. The contentions of his times increased to him the difficulty of perceiving what formed the substance of Christianity itself. Yet whatever place he may himself have occupied, he rendered considerable services to Christianity. Some of these have already been occasionally mentioned; it might suffice to add that he restored the key to the right understanding of the Old Testament, as the preliminary education[2] of the human race, and removed the superficial objections against the particularism of the earlier revelation, and the omission of a future state; and which was yet more important, the change which he mainly produced in the too abstract sys-

---

[1] In his essay über die Natürliche Religion he explains Christianity by means of Pantheism.

[2] In his concise but deep and much-containing essay, " über die Erziehung des Menschengeschlechts." A Christian would indeed defend some things differently, and the Pantheistic scheme lies as the basis; it has, however, much that is valuable.

tems of evidence of the then Apologists, and his referring to the Bible itself as its own best, or, as he held, its only, advocate [1]. He further, in opposition to a presumptuous philosophy, pointed out the limits of the empire of reason, by admitting, that though reason must decide whether a given system be a revelation or no, yet if it find in that revelation things which it cannot explain, this should rather determine it for it than against it. Lessing, however, though he exerted a considerable influence upon Theology, came only incidentally in contact with it; the dryness, with which it was cultivated at Leipzig, whither he was in his youth sent to study, seems to have deterred him from making it a professional pursuit. The services also which he rendered were, it seems, rather external to Christianity, in preparing the way for a higher order of Christian apologetic authors, than any direct illustrations of its truths. Herder, on the other hand, though, from the predominance of imagination in his mental character, his own views were rather dim and distant conceptions, than any full realizations of the truths which flashed across, rather than dwelt upon his mind, promoted variously their subsequent reception; the natural simplicity and deep feeling of his mind enabled him, partially at least, to understand much of the deeper contents of the Chris-

---

[1] The only book, says Lessing often in his controversy with Göze, which is, properly speaking, written in behalf of the truth of the Bible, or which can be written for it, is the Bible itself.

tian documents, which the satisfied self-sufficiency of his contemporaries had pronounced to be the mere temporary disguise of the eternal truths of reason: through his genuine oriental spirit he was enabled to penetrate and to shew the fuller meaning of much in the Old Testament, which their partial and unhistorical rationalism had neglected or despised, as mythos or unmeaning exaggeration. The entire insight which Christian experience would have given, was indeed here also wanting; his early education by one of a repulsive, gloomy, and austere spirit, had alienated his mind, of which feeling and imagination were the chief characteristics, from the more earnest contemplation of Christianity; his natural character, strengthened by this alienation and by his devotion to classical literature and the belles-lettres, led him to view it chiefly on its æsthetik-moral side, to defend it from its loveliness rather than as the only way to holiness. Still, amid this generally mistaken direction of his endeavours, a susceptible mind, as Herder's, could not but frequently be penetrated with a deeper consciousness; and accordingly, not merely in his earlier works [1], before the love of reputation made him imperceptibly enter into a compromise with the spirit of his times, is there much useful, many a sentiment full

---

[1] Such are especially die älteste Urkunde des Menschengeschlechts; die Briefe das Studium der Theologie betreffend; die Anmerkungen zum N. T. aus einer neueröffneten morgenländischer Quelle.

of Christian meaning, and much correct conception, but even in his later writings, where every thing seems to float in a dim mist, so that a contemporary[1] compared them to a distant cloud, of which one could not distinguish whether it were a cloud, or a city with inhabitants, is many a hint, which may be pursued to clearer and enlarged views.

These men, however, wrote principally for a succeeding generation; their own age was too deeply stamped with its empiric-rationalistic character, to be much alive to minds so unlike their own. A deep impression was first made by one, who, in the province of philosophy itself, shewed the nothingness of the boasted pretences of the popular philosophy, to build a system on the grounds of 'sound human reason.' Before Kant, German philosophy had been content to speculate, without entering into the previous question, how far human reason is capable of attaining any certain knowledge in things not cognizable by the senses. This enquiry Kant was induced by the scepticism of Hume to institute, and the result to which his investigations led him was, that " speculative intellect " cannot prove that the ideas, at which it arrives, are more than ideas, that its objects have any objective, independent, existence[2]. Speculative intellect then failing, Kant

---

[1] Garve.
[2] The object of Kant's enquiry was, wherein consists the constitution of our mental nature previous to all experience, what in

tried the way of practical intellect. Here he found as an absolute universal principle, the 'categorical imperative' in man, the consciousness of a fundamental law in his nature, that he ought to realize that which is prescribed by the moral law, so that the maxims of his will on each occasion might serve as the principles of an universal legis-

it exists purely, or a priori? The three fundamental powers of mind, by which ideas are conveyed to us, are, according to his Kritik der reinen Vernunft, perception, understanding, and intellect. In perception, all which exists a priori, is time and space: these however are merely conditions of our power of contemplating external objects; exterior to us they are nothing. Understanding is, according to Kant, the power of reducing the manifold objects of perception under generic heads. The summa genera of these (the Categories) in that they comprize all the objects of perception, introduce unity and connection into the subjects of contemplation; and thence results experience. Intellect, lastly, embraces the pure conceptions, which lie beyond all experience, called ideas. Of these the most universal, the highest and purest, is the Unconditional and Absolute. Of this there are three classes: 1. The absolute unity of the recipient of the impressions, when detached from all accidents. 2. The absolute unity of all $\varphi a\iota\nu\acute{o}\mu\varepsilon\nu a$, in the whole succession in which they are presented. 3. The absolute unity of all objects of conception. In the first of these respects, the fundamental idea of the intellect is Psycologic, and denotes the soul; in the second Cosmologic, and denotes the world; in the third Theologic, and denotes God. These three ideas, he proceeded, which are merely subjective and relative, had been considered as something objective, as objects existing external to ourselves, and thereupon had been constructed a rational Psycology, a transcendental Cosmology, and a natural Theology; in a word, metaphysic: sciences, the existence of whose object cannot be proved, in that 'speculative intellect' cannot shew that these ideas are more than ideas.

lation. This universal principle, it appeared, exists independently of any thing external; its universality Kant assumes as an established fact; that every rational being namely is conscious of this unconditional unlimited law, and then most strongly, when his inclinations are in contradiction to it. If then this law have a real existence, in order that practical intellect may not be in contradiction with itself, it must have a right to assume as postulates whatever is necessary to its reality. These postulates are, according to Kant, free-agency, immortality, and the existence of a personal God. Free agency, as the indispensable condition of all morality; immortality, because if this law really exist in man, there must be a capability of its realization; but man can only make an imperfect approach to its full realization in this life, therefore there must be a continued personal existence, during which he may make an endless approach to the highest degree of it, perfect holiness. This law further, though it admit of nothing exterior to itself as a motive to its completion, comprises in the idea of its fulfilment the idea of happiness proportionate to the degree of its fulfilment, and consequently requires the existence of a perfect moral being, Author and Governor of the world, who should allot this blessedness. In brief, that if there be no God, no free agency, no immortality, this law will involve a contradiction.

The present is not the place to point out the defects in the postulates of this system, in consequence of which it was afterwards overthrown, but solely the influences of the system itself upon Theology. These were for the time injurious, but permanently beneficial. Its ill effects resulted from its positive side; the idea of God was lowered, and became grossly anthropomorphic, in that he appeared to exist not for himself, but in order to allot the degree of blessedness, which man by his compliance with the moral law might deserve. The moral law occupied the place of, and became, God: all the relations of man to God, (except as far as he was the distributer of rewards) and consequently all prayer, ceased: a cold intellectual system of dry morality was substituted consequently for religion. Especially pernicious was the (only short lived) system of moral interpretation, by which Kantian moral ideas were substituted for Christian doctrine. Kant, though he held that the belief of pure reason was the only foundation of an universal and true Church, saw that a Church could only be actually erected among mankind through a positive revealed legislation, that there must consequently be an historical Church-belief: " This however must be united to the 'moral belief' by an uniform interpretation in a sense which agrees with the universal practical rules of a pure religion of reason." This interpretation, he confessed, might often appear, often be, forced, if considered in relation to the text of the revelation; yet must it be preferred to the literal, which contained merely theoretical truth. The only real truth according to

Kant, is such as can be found in human reason; what lays beyond it could be no object of conception, and therefore must be prejudicial to man, in that it would make him neglect known truths to pursue unknown [1]. The old error of the Gnostical interpreters in the early Church was thus revived, an example set for the subsequent identification of Scripture doctrine with the results of speculation, and, for the time, the Scriptures valued only as the vehicle, the Founder of Christianity only as far as he was a teacher, of morals analagous to that of Kant. This mode of exposition, however, though for the time theoretically much approved, was precluded from any permanent practical ascendancy, by the firmness which the historical-grammatical interpretation had now acquired. It exerted, however, finally a salutary

---

[1] This system was contained in his " Die Religion innerhalb der Gränzen der reinen Vernunft." According to this theory, the doctrine of the Trinity became symbolical of the three fundamental points of universal religion, that there is a holy law-giver, a holy benefactor, a holy retributor; the doctrine that " the blood of Christ makes us pure," yielding, according to the views of this school, no practical results, the blood as containing the vital principle, was to be explained of the life, and the meaning of the expression was to be, that when, through a community of life with Christ, his life had penetrated and united itself with ours, and we had conformed ours to his, we became pure. The moral practical feeling, or tact, was in each case to supply the practical result, where the point in revelation did not furnish it; none such being e. g. to be obtained, according to these theorists, from the curses upon David's enemies, this moral tact was to perceive that under these enemies were designated his passions.

influence on that system, by recalling the important principle of the Reformation, that a bare stiff philology, or an historical knowledge, which perpetually hovered around without ever reaching its object, were no sufficient keys to the meaning of Scripture. It cannot, on the other hand, be considered a disadvantage, that rationalism, which had before been a desultory aggregate of mere negations, began to assume a definite and scientific shape: a philosophic basis was indeed thereby given to the *à priori* objections against miracles and prophecy; yet the temporary evil was more than counterbalanced by the attempt to construct a system of its own; since the more it attempts this, the more visible will ever become the superiority of Revelation, the more manifest its own intrinsic emptiness. The benefits conferred by the Kantian philosophy resulted more immediately from its negative, ultimately also from its positive, side; from the former, not only by the destruction of the Wolfian demonstrative method, and the annihilation of the presumptuous shallowness of the popular philosophy, but in that by shewing the inadequacy of speculative reason in matters uncognizable by sense, it led many, who were not bound by the fetters of the new philosophy, to listen to the voice of nature, the revelation of God within them, and to seek as the direct result of consciousness, the truths which speculation was unable scientifically to justify; a course, which it was expected by many[1] that

[1] See Immanuel ein Buch für Juden und Heiden. Berlin 1802.

Kant himself must have adopted. Nor is there any point at which the mind, which had resolved upon this step, could consistently rest, short of the acceptance of Christianity itself. On its positive side, the uncompromising strictness, with which it pronounced the full and complete realization of the perfect moral law to be the fundamental principle of our nature, re-awakened the moral consciousness from the slumber into which it had been cast by the enervating system of Eudaimonism; and though man wearied himself for a while in the endeavour to fulfil this law in his own strength, the more vivid the perception of its claims became, and the more that man was in consequence disquieted through the inadequacy of his own fulfilment of them, the more earnest must be the longing after a higher assistance, after a reconciliation with himself and with his God: the "Categorical Imperative," was, as the law of old, an initiating instructor which led him to Christ[1]. The fuller acquaintance with the moral nature of man, at which this philosophy arrived through a more persevering speculation upon the human mind, shewed also, especially in the acknowledgment of an in-dwelling disposition to evil, that a deeper philosophy was more in harmony with the depth of Christian truth[2]. A preparatory education, however, on

---

[1] Twesten, S. 218.
[2] The first treatise in his " Die Religion innerhalb der Gränzen der reinen Vernunft," is on " the radical evil of Human Nature;"

an extensive scale must be slow; and the Kantian philosophy reigned for a considerable time undisputed and unmodified in every department of science[1]. History and doctrinal theology were alike under its sway, and suffered for the time the more from the absoluteness of the dominion by which it enchained the mind. Yet where this system was comprehended in its depth, and not merely verbally followed, it did evince its tendency to produce a return to the essential truths of the Gospel, as in one Theologian especially, whom Kant esteemed among his best disciples and his friend[2].

Additional energy and activity of mind was produced by a bold disciple of Kant, who completing Kant's system on its negative side by a correct inference, which it is strange that Kant

the second on the claims of the good principle to the dominion over man; the similar claims of the evil principle, the struggle between them, and what the New Testament teaches of man's fall into sin, and of the means by which he may free himself from the dominion of the evil principle.

[1] Hamann, (a man whose worth was not appreciated by his contemporaries, but who possessed a very philosophic as well as religious mind), and Herder especially, complain of the dry scholastic method which this system introduced, as did Johann. von Müller with reference to history.

[2] Stäudlin, who first treated the system of Christian doctrine on the principles of Kant, which, however, he by no means servilely followed. The doctrinal theologians of the pure critical philosophy, were chiefly Tieftrunck at Halle, 1791—6, Schmidt. at Jena, 1797, and Ammon at Göttingen, 1797; who, however, in the later form of his work, the Summa Theologiæ Christianæ, 1803, employed it only negatively. Schröckh, 43, 65—71.

himself overlooked, founded thereon his own. The groundwork of Fichte's system was the same as Berkeley's. If, according to Kant, the predicaments which we ascribe to things are merely the results of our own subjective impressions, and we know not what the things in themselves are, but they are an unknown quantity, which the human mind has invested with properties, according to the necessary laws under which it contemplates them, it was an obvious question, how do we know that such things exist at all, exterior to our own minds, that this unknown quantity is more than the qualities which result from the laws of the human mind? The conclusion of Fichte then was, that the whole material world has no existence exterior to ourselves, that it only appears to us to exist in consequence of certain laws of our mind. This material appearance he accounted for, from the essential nature of the human mind. God, according to him, the infinite Ens, exists through the finite thought of finite spirits. Finite thought is the existence and image of the infinite Ens. Finite thought, however, if limited to itself, would be dissipated and become a nothing; to give it reality and life, there must be a contrast in itself; hence infinite thought, coming into existence in finite, places together with thought a something, by which thought may be confined. This is the material world, which appears as something external, so that with each self is necessarily united a not-self, a contrast to self. The life and activity of human thought consists then, in a continued endeavour to break through that by which it is confined, partly theoretically, by penetrating and thinking through the objects, and thus appropriating them to thought, and as it were, converting them into it; partly practically, by raising itself above all the laws of the not-self, so that man lives from and for himself. This system was useful in producing energy, yet this energy was in the first instance confined to abstract thought, and it engendered a proud high-mindedness both theoretically and practically; theoretically in the contempt of all material science, of every thing but abstract thought, practically in that it attributed to man a freedom which belongs only to God, and thereby produced a most unbounded egotism [1].

A new element was introduced into Germany by the nature-philosophy of Schelling. Fichte had endeavoured to solve the contrast of matter and spirit by denying the existence of the former, and transferring the contrast to the mind; Schelling's problem was to remove it essentially. He attributed as real an existence to the material as to the ideal empire of things, so that the empire of material things was only a different mode of expression of the immaterial. Spirit, by thinking matter through, frees it as it were from its con-

---

[1] Fichte's system may be collected best from Fichte'ns Appellation an das Publicum über die ihm beigefügte Beschuldigung des Atheismus, 1791. Anweisung zum seligen Leben, 1806. Schelling's Darlegung des wahren Verhältnisses der Naturphilosophie zur verbesserten Fichte'schen Lehre. 1806.

finement, in that it looses its spirit. In that; however, the laws of matter are the expression of spirit, the spirit only becomes conscious of itself, in that it thinks matter through and appropriates it; so that the whole employment of speculation upon external things is only a self-affirmation. God accordingly cannot be considered as a mere unity, but can only be conceived as a living God, in that he has a contrast in himself; the removal of which is his life. The unity of God has consequently continually revealed itself in plurality, spirit in matter, that the plurality may extricate itself into unity, matter be exalted to spirit, and be freed. The system of Schelling produced indirectly as well as directly a great revolution; while the activity and independence of mind, which it much contributed to rouse, precluded those parts within itself, from which danger might be apprehended to the Christian system, from exerting that universal influence which the Kantian philosophy had exercised, it excited a vivid consciousness of the universal presence and agency of a living and infinite being; and thereby overthrow the dead barren idea of an epicurean deity at a distance from, and without connection with, the world, and the unworthy deduction of the infinite from the finite. By the introduction of contemplation, instead of mere abstract thought, it awakened a deeper mode of seeking after knowledge than was admitted by the previous systems; and in the direct province of theology it acknowledged, or introduced, that susceptibility for truths beyond the compass of intellectual speculation, which those systems had effaced. " It has partly again acknowledged, in part it has, though dimly, anticipated a deeper meaning in the ideas of the Christian Theology, which had been entirely concealed from the common view. To many it has been a point of transition to a Christian conviction; to many it has restored the courage to undertake a scientific defence of Christianity, and has exerted an influence favourable to it even upon systems at variance with itself[1]."

Jacobi acknowledged the consistency of these systems, as also of Pantheism, but could not acquiesce in their results; he therefore opposed to them the doctrine of immediate consciousness in divine things. He maintained that there must be an immediate certainty of knowledge in regard to the deity, (whether it be termed feeling, or consciousness, or intellect,) whereas speculation only arrived at this knowledge immediately: that this immediate consciousness taught man to believe in God, as a being different from and in contrast with himself, in the freedom of man, in personal continued-existence, and in the objective existence of evil[2]. The part

---

[1] Twesten, S. 198. who instances Fichte; comp. Schelling, Verhältniss der Naturphilosophie zur verbesserten Fichte'schen Lehre Tüb. 1806. This system was itself but little directly admitted into doctrinal theology; the above-mentioned work of Daub is the only instance; and even that (according to Twest. S. 200.) is among the most visible proofs of the commenced independence of doctrinal theology from the schools to which the authors are addicted.

[2] See especially his Einleitung über Göttliche Dinge.

of Jacobi's system unfavourable to revelation was the extension of the same principle to historical information, as being equally mediate with speculation, and therefore as little capable of conveying real knowledge. Jacobi accordingly accepted only the idea of the truths of revelation, not their historical basis. He forgot that his four truths are no where to be found, exterior to Christianity, as indeed through it they first acquire their practical importance; he failed to perceive the ground of this fact, that though the acknowledgment of his truths does lie deep in human nature, in consequence of its yet remaining likeness to the divine, they must now be cleared up by the aid of Revelation, and that to man in his present state, other truths beyond these four are necessary.

The latest form of rationalism established itself as the result of these systems; but from these same systems has its untenableness, both in its positive and negative sides, been beyond all question established; and in its strictest contrast to revelation it has nearly disappeared [1]. The support which it before claimed for its positive contents from speculation or from "sound human reason," has been withdrawn by the overthrow of the Wolfian and Popular Philosophy; the most of its adherents built therefore, (though in a very different spirit from its excellent author) on

[1] Among theologians, the only remaining adherents of any note of the strict rationalistic school are Wegscheider and Rohr.

the principle of Jacobi, on consciousness as the source of knowledge in divine things, and thereby disabled themselves from effectually attacking the believer in revelation, or from defending themselves against the Pantheist. Of the believer in revelation they could no longer require, that he should establish by reason truths which lie beyond reason, since they confessed themselves, that they could not establish by reason free-agency, human personality, &c. which they yet continued to hold; the Pantheist on the other hand maintained against the rationalist, as he did against the believer in revelation, that the unproved truths of the deist were merely the product of subjective self-deception, derived from the ascription of human qualities and human feelings to the deity. The shallowness of his conceptions of moral evil, which produced his denial both of the original declension of man, and of the necessity of the means for his restoration, which Christianity contains, were exposed by the system of Kant: the anthropomorphic views of God, as a mechanical contriver of the world, which, like the human author of a machine, he was imagined subsequently to have left to carry on the work for which it was designed, (on which views the distinctions between the mediate and immediate agency of God, the so-called interruptions of the laws of nature, &c. and the consequent criticisms of revelation were founded,) were annihilated by the philosophy of Schelling. The rest of the system of rationalism was too mere an abstraction of Christianity, deprived of its radiancy and warmth, long to endure ; its criticisms of revelation the same as those which our invaluable Butler has shewn can be consistently urged only by the Atheist or the Pantheist. That milder form, which, according to the scholastic distinction, admits things above, but not those contrary to, human reason [1], rather incidentally and occasionally, than in its own nature, agrees with the pure Rationalism, and stands within or without Scriptural Christianity, according as the Christian doctrines appear to each individual who adopts it, contrary or not to that reason ; but even among those, who on this ground yet remain strangers to the main Christian doctrines, there exists, in very many at least, that deep moral earnestness, which must in time bring them to their acknowledgment.

The final issue of this great developement is yet too incomplete, the extensive re-animation of a living Christianity too recent, the degrees in and the forms under which it has often been restored, too various, to allow a stranger now to pronounce upon either the causes or the extent of

[1] The reality of this distinction has been questioned by some moderns, as if what was above, were also contrary to, reason ; yet " not to belong to, not to be within the province of," is no more equivalent to the "being opposed to," than " not to love," is " to hate." In saying that a thing is contrary to reason, we acknowledge that it lies within the cognizance of that faculty ; in saying that a subject is above it, we ascribe to it a different order of things, for which reason has no criterion.

that restoration, or to express any opinions upon the individuals who have been, under providence, the means of that restoration. From the very advanced state of theological education in Germany, a vast influence is at all times in active agency, of which no conception can be formed either from its printed literature, or from a residence at a limited number of universities. By far the largest portion of German Theology is a floating capital; so that no just estimate can be made from the printed works of any theologian, of the extent or variety of his usefulness, while a great proportion will always remain, who are the instruments of a widely diffused blessing, to which their embodied theology bears not the remotest proportion: still more difficult is it for a stranger, especially for one, who has only witnessed in his own country a scrupulous adherence to a received system, to see how far much which is contrary to his own views may not only not be injurious, but, in a different state of things, even beneficial to the essentials of Christianity. Much that appears to be dangerous in a system, which has not been in all its parts deeply examined, is found in a more advanced stage to be useful or necessary: the wind, which might be fatal within a narrow channel, serves only to bear onward more prosperously in its way the vessel which has taken a freer and a bolder course.

Without however venturing to define the causes, or name the instruments of this great renovation, the gains of this long and perilous career are in part obvious; the banishment of a reliance upon the mere letter of a received system, of a mere intellectual conception of Christianity, of a deadening formularism, of the undervaluing of Scripture in behalf of an over-refined human system, of an uncharitable polemic, which partly rivetted the attention upon mere collateral or subordinate points, partly obliterated the import of the most momentous truths; (acting as these evils did on practical as well as scientific theology), and the renewed and energetic life given by the opposite of all these aberrations, are on the purely religious side an immeasurable, inestimable, gain; on the scientific side the principles established in each theological science, and its more comprehensive and juster cultivation, have been productive of yet greater benefit to theology than even the enlarged and correcter knowledge, which has resulted from the continued investigations produced by these collisions; many theories (as those on the principles of interpretation) which were partially developed by different minds, and injurious while partial, have in their more enlarged application become favourable to the purer development of Scriptural truth: many weak points, which before were stumbling-blocks in the reception either of Revelation or of the essentials of Christianity, have been removed or replaced: it has indeed been necessary to examine deeply the foundations of Christianity, but thereby has the rock upon which it rests, been again discovered from amid the accumulation of human theories by which it was concealed, but which yielded to the first shock of the storm or the flood: while in the well-founded confidence, which past experience has given to the German enquirer, there is a rich promise, that the already commenced blending of belief and science, without which science becomes dead, and belief is exposed to degeneracy, will be perfected beyond even the degree to which it was realized in some of the noblest instruments of the earlier Reformation. Nor is it any slight advantage (compared to its earlier state) that no investigation is now entered upon with that hesitating timidity, which contemplates the results with reference only to an existing human system, thereby producing an unconscious bias to blink the difficulties by which the wished-for conclusion is opposed, and becoming unsusceptible for that portion of truth, which may exist in a scheme at variance with one's own. Controversy, whether within or without Christianity, would have been spared much of its bitterness, have been sooner ended, and produced richer and earlier results, had this candour been more uniformly exercised.

How soon these great results may be fully realized can be known only to Him, " in whose power are the times and seasons" of his Church. Yet in contemplating the probability of their arrival, it must be recollected that the individuals employed in their acceleration must be weighed, not counted; that every individual who has extricated himself from the mazes of unbelief, as many of these have done, is not only a witness to others of the living force of Christianity, but is himself so much the firmer and more energetic a minister of the faith which he has won; that many, who themselves still stand short of a perfect Scriptural faith, are yet in various measures and degrees engaged in promoting its final renovation; that there may be the same Christian feeling in very different forms of expression, or that the basis may exist, though the intellectual developement of it may be impeded by the intricacies of an earlier-admitted system of philosophy [1]; and that, in the sceptical struggle after truth, of many who are yet in doubt with regard either to the essential doctrines of Christianity, or to revelation itself, there may be often more of the Christian spirit, than in an unhesitating traditionary belief. The final issue of this crisis may be impeded by a mistaken political interference, which can now only create re-action, or engender hypocrites; or, in a lesser degree, by the distractions and irregularities produced by the intervention of foreign religious bodies [2]; yet it seems neither too san-

[1] Though the mention of living authors has been for the most part purposely avoided, one may, it is believed, safely instance De Wette, as one whose really Christian faith is only obscured by his adherence to the Friesian Philosophy.

[2] From the author's personal knowledge of Germany and from the views of some very Christian practical clergy of that country, of whom he enquired, he is strongly assured that such interference

guine nor presumptuous to hope that the time is not far distant when the religious energy, now widely visible in Germany, shall produce its fruits, and the Evangelical Church, strengthened by the increasing internal unanimity, fortified against error by past experience, and founded on a Scriptural faith, shall again, in religious as well as scientific depth, be at least one amongst the fairest

---

could only retard the object which it wishes to promote; that it would not only increase the suspicions of Sectarianism and Schism, under which the revival of a living Christianity has already been calumniated, but that it would necessarily introduce disorder and division, and might both occasion direct political interference, render individual opposition more plausible, and alienate the undiscriminating. It is perhaps a natural feeling in a time of strong excitement, for each individual to think that too much cannot be done, or that his own exertions if earnest cannot be misapplied; and in this country especially, a feeling, analogous to that energetically described by the Greek historian, seems to be revived, that nothing can be well done which English piety and English charity are not concerned in promoting. The author doubts not the goodness of the motives of the members of the " Continental Society ;" but it might be well if they would re-consider whether their interference is not likely to produce a diminution of Christian charity, whether it be in itself justifiable, and whether it would not imply a firmer faith in Him, who has promised never to desert his Church, to leave the German Church under the care of those pastors whom He has raised up in it, instead of intruding, uncalled, into a foreign fold. The author must repeat that the statement of these sentiments arises not from any doubt of the piety of the objects of the Continental Society, whose members are personally unknown to him, but from the conviction that their exertions in Germany are unnecessary, and would be prejudicial.

portions of the universal Church of the Redeemer.

It may be permitted, in confirmation of these hopes, to present the view given by the valuable author, already so often quoted[1], remarking only, that Theologians form but a very small proportion of the second class described, and that as Theology was the last department which felt the influence of the inroad of unbelief, so likewise has it naturally been the first to recover itself; that moreover, even as far as Theology is pre-eminently considered in any portion of this picture, the view of the author, from the character of his own mind and the nature of his subject, seems principally to have been directed to those developements, in which philosophy has been most influential, and where a pure renovation of Christian faith, though often deeper, would perhaps in its own nature be slower; and that one may be justified, therefore, in forming brighter expectations of an earlier conclusion, than he in the midst of the struggle has ventured to anticipate.

" The mass of the Lutheran Church, the people namely, as they were but little affected by the defects of the old Theology, so have they also been by the revolutions of the new[2]; if there have been at-

---

[1] Twesten, S. 216—220.

[2] The author may be permitted to remark in confirmation, that he has heard more than one sermon founded upon rationalist principles, and stating incidentally rationalist views, of which he had

tempts to adapt it to them, yet have not the innovations been able to penetrate either very deeply or very generally; the people has, on the whole, remained true and attached to the faith of their fathers. The religious ideas seem indeed to have lost in strength and efficacy; the habits, the whole form of domestic and public life no longer express

reason to know that the positive evil passed by wholly unperceived by the congregations; in several cases where these had been more prominently promulged, the congregations had, through their own biblical knowledge, been able to correct them, and in some had even insisted on the removal of their preacher. In general, however, the effects of rationalism upon the pulpit were solely to produce dry moral discourses, or if a different meaning were attached and attributed by the preacher to the doctrinal terms which he yet retained, the congregations, in whom their former faith was kept alive by the study of the Scripture, and the hymns of a more pious age which Germany possesses in such rich abundance, continued to understand them in their original Christian meaning. Among the lower classes, the unchristian publications, directly manufactured for them, found but little access; and the author was informed, on enquiring upon this subject, in one Prussian University where the lowest class could without exception read, that the Bible and the Hymn-book were alone actually read. It may be added, that in several places where an attempt has been made to substitute new hymns for the public use, in which the Christian doctrines were modernized, or omitted, it has been successfully resisted by the congregations. It is, however, upon the whole, due to the German clergy to state, that though there may have been some flagrant instances of the violation of pastoral duty, the defects have not, upon the whole, been different in kind from those, which have often resulted from a dead orthodoxism; the effects have been negative rather than positive, rather the withholding of more nutritious, than the substitution of unwholesome, food.

the same uniform reference to the Christian ideas, which they formerly did: worldly-mindedness, deficiency in faith and in piety, may have gained ground; yet perhaps it is only, that what formerly lay concealed under a scrupulous adherence to forms now displays itself more openly. Let but the evangelical faith again be energetically preached, the evangelical congregations will appear more readily than many now dare to hope. Not so much a reanimation as a new arousing of the already existing life is necessary; it is a condition like that of the chrysalis in the coverings of the pupa; the old formations have been dissolved, the anatomist sees within the larva nothing but shapeless matter; yet there do lie within it the preparations for a new organization, wherewith the being, unfolded into a higher class, goes forth from its envelopements.

"With regard to the learned and cultivated classes, at least a certain tolerance towards the faith of the Church has revived, among many a reverence and a need of it. It has been perceived, that the way which has been hitherto trod led to no blessing; the illumination has not produced its vaunted fruits; philosophy has not justified the confidence with which it was exultingly greeted; after the foundation of positive faith had been undermined, in many, very many, the general truths of the so-called natural religion sunk in the ruins; the unsatisfactoriness of a scepticism is now felt, which conceals itself perchance under loud-sounding phrases, but deceives not the experienced, who has been tried in the struggles of life, and which deserts its adherent without consolation in the presence of death. We have become convinced, that by the side of the many systems, which in part without any great expenditure of intellect and of originality, have yet found approbation or been tolerated amongst us, that of the old Church, which is inferior to no other in consistency and depth, may with honour maintain its place; whoever consequently undertakes to defend it, has at least (with the exception of a few journals and a few individuals, the representatives of an earlier period), no longer to anticipate the common contempt and the hostility of all the self-deemed wise; and if the larger number, like the Athenians of old, (Acts xvii.) reserve the further investigation for another time, yet is there here and there another Dionysius the Areopagite among them, who finds here what he had hitherto sought in vain.

" It must further be acknowledged, that even among those who yet remain estranged to the faith, the respect for moral duty, the feeling for what is good and noble has not diminished; rather has it been animated and elevated by that very philosophy, to which the majority of the opponents of the ancient system of the Church is attached. Those who deny or doubt every thing else, deny not that morality determines the worth of man; there is no one who would not be ashamed of a theory which regarded duty as subordinate to interest, virtue to enjoyment. Moral systems, which refer morality to the mere impulse after well-being, would now meet with no success: the taste of the age has withdrawn even from favourite authors, who seemed to sanction less strict principles. This moral earnestness which animates all men of the better order among us, is an important point for the preacher of Evangelical Christianity, with which to connect its truths; for their reception depends upon a moral disposition; the stricter the system of morality becomes, the less can there fail a feeling of the necessity of reconciliation and of a higher assistance, which can only be realized in Christ: as the law formerly, so may now the categorical imperative be a preparatory instructor to lead to Christ.

" To this must be added, what we have before mentioned, the more favourable direction which science has taken. Mere empiricism and materialism have vanished from the schools of philosophy; the religious ideas are indeed differently explained and interpreted, but they are acknowledged every where; the disposition has ceased to ascribe reality only to that which admits of demonstration; the understanding and the will are no longer accounted the only modes in which the activity of the mental powers can exert itself; the claims of the feeling, the peculiar organ of religion in man, remain no longer unregarded.

" On the other hand a different spirit is aroused in historical studies also. The time is past in which Christian antiquity furnished materials only for the exercise of critical acumen, with which there was no sympathy, from which the mind was too estranged to be able to obtain from it a pure historical picture; the mind has ceased to be susceptible only for what coincides with certain prevailing opinions; it has learnt the abstraction from self, necessary for the full reception of the impressions of history. Much has thus become intelligible to us, which hitherto was as a sealed book, and in the same proportion has it been brought nearer to us; we feel ourselves attracted by the character and the efforts of antiquity; we can transport ourselves into their feelings and modes of conception; we can derive pleasure and improvement from the expressions of their Christian sentiments. By these means has that pride been checked, through which our age deemed itself raised so far above every thing which preceded it; what our ancestors have transmitted to us as the fruit of their exertions, is no more rejected without further examination as valueless; but the duty of respecting, and of faithfully preserving it, is acknowledged, wherever it was not founded on transient circumstances of the time, but expressed the fundamental ideas of Christianity and Protestantism. At the same time, however, the investigations in Scriptural interpretation and in history have cleared away much, which hindered the right understanding and free appropriation of these ideas; the essential has been separated from the non-essential and accidental, the indifferent and unimportant has been brought back to its true value; the genuine traits of Evangelical Christianity are become more clearly prominent, since that has been removed through which it was thought to help out, or to adorn, the portrait; so that there is nothing to deter any one from accepting it, in whom there is found an internal alliance with its spirit.

"The ground then is prepared; it remains only that the seed of a living faith be cast into it. The fields are ready to harvest; only may the Lord of the harvest send his labourers! And why should we not put our trust in him, who has planted, propagated, preserved Christianity among circumstances so much more difficult? He, whose assistance our Church has experienced in so many a severe contest, will not desert it even now, whether he presently send one, who in the spirit and power of a Luther shall quickly turn the hearts, and bring back the minds of the fathers to the children, or whether it lie in his purpose that the crisis shall slowly unfold itself, and the religious life should gradually recover a sound and healthy state. Many appearances of the times point to a deeper, more universal, awakening of belief. If this be derived from the right source, then in a short time the undecided will become determined; the wavering, firm; the cold, warm; the lukewarm be borne along; and those foreign intermixtures be separated, which here and there create a suspicion of the good cause even in the minds of the well-disposed, and give to the adversaries a plausible ground of depreciating or of opposing it."

THE END.

Printed by R. GILBERT, St. John's Square, London.

NEW WORKS

PRINTED FOR

C. AND J. RIVINGTON,

ST. PAUL'S CHURCH-YARD, AND WATERLOO-PLACE, PALL-MALL.

I.

BIOGRAPHICAL NOTICES of the APOSTLES, EVANGELISTS, and other SAINTS. With Reflections adapted to the Minor Festivals of the Church. By the Right Rev. RICHARD MANT, D.D. Lord Bishop of Down and Connor. 8vo. 13s.

II.

LECTURES on the CRITICISM and INTERPRETATION of the BIBLE, with two Preliminary Lectures on Theological Study and Theological Arrangement: to which are now added, Two LECTURES on the History of Biblical Interpretation. *New Edition;* corrected. By HERBERT MARSH, D.D. F.R.S. and F.S.A. Lady Margaret's Professor of Divinity in the University of Cambridge and Bishop of Peterborough. 8vo. 14s.

** This Volume contains the four first Parts of his Lordship's Course of Lectures: the fifth, sixth, and seventh Parts may be had, in continuation, price 7s.

III.

THE HISTORY of the REFORMATION of the CHURCH of ENGLAND. By HENRY SOAMES, M.A. Rector of Shelley, Essex. In Four large Volumes. 8vo. 3l. 4s.

IV.

An INTRODUCTION to the WRITINGS of the NEW TESTAMENT. By Dr. JOHN LEONARD HUG, Professor of Theology in the University of Freyburgh. Translated from the German, with an Introduction and Notes by the Rev. DANIEL GUILFORD WAIT, LL.D. Rector of Blagdon and Member of the Royal Asiatic Society. In Two large Volumes. 8vo. 1l. 12s.

V.

RECENSIO SYNOPTICA ANNOTATIONIS SACRÆ: Or CRITICAL DIGEST of the most important ANNOTATIONS, Exegetical, Philological, and Theological, on the New Testament. By the Rev. S. T. BLOOMFIELD, A.M. Vicar of Bisbrook, Rutland. In Eight large Volumes. 8vo. 6l. 2s.

New Works published by C. and J. Rivington.

VI.

The CONNECTION of SACRED and PROFANE HISTORY, from the Death of Joshua until the Decline of the Kingdoms of Israel and Judah. (Intended to complete the Works of SHUCKFORD and PRIDEAUX.) By the Rev. M. RUSSELL, LL.D. Episcopal Minister, Leith. In Two Volumes. 8vo. 1*l*. 8*s*.

VII.

HORÆ CATECHETICÆ; or an Exposition of the Duty and Advantages of PUBLIC CATECHISING in CHURCH. In a Letter to the LORD BISHOP of LONDON. By W. S. GILLY, M.A. Prebendary of Durham; and Perpetual Curate of St. Margaret's, Durham. Small 8vo. 5*s*. 6*d*.

Also, by the same Author,

A FOURTH EDITION of a NARRATIVE of an EXCURSION to the MOUNTAINS of PIEMONT in 1823; with Ten Views of Scenery and two large Maps. 8vo. 18*s*.

⁎⁎⁎ The Ten Views may be purchased separately, price 6*s*.

VIII.

PAROCHIAL SERMONS, illustrative of the Importance of the Revelation of GOD in JESUS CHRIST. By the Rev. RENN D. HAMPDEN, A.M. late Fellow of Oriel College, Oxford. 12mo. 7*s*. 6*d*.

IX.

A SERIES of DISCOURSES on the STATE of the PROTESTANT RELIGION in GERMANY. Preached before the University of Cambridge, in 1825. Second Edition. (In the Press.) By HUGH JAMES ROSE, B.D. Vicar of Horsham, Sussex. 8vo.

Also, by the same Author,

An APPENDIX to the foregoing; being a REPLY to the German Critiques on that Work. 8vo. 3*s*. 6*d*.

X.

The APOCALYPSE of ST. JOHN, or PROPHECY of the Rise, Progress, and Fall of the Church of Rome; the Inquisition; the French Revolution; the Universal War; and the final Triumph of Christianity. Being a new Interpretation. Second Edition. By the Rev. GEORGE CROLY, A.M. H.R.S.L. 8vo. 12*s*.

ImTheStory.com

Personalized Classic Books in many genre's

Unique gift for kids, partners, friends, colleagues

Customize:

- Character Names
- Upload your own front/back cover images (optional)
- Inscribe a personal message/dedication on the inside page (optional)

Customize many titles Including
- Alice in Wonderland
- Romeo and Juliet
- The Wizard of Oz
- A Christmas Carol
- Dracula
- Dr. Jekyll & Mr. Hyde
- And more...

Emily's Adventures in Wonderland

Ryan & Julia

Printed by BoD™in Norderstedt, Germany